lonely planet

BEIJING
ENCOUNTER

DAVID EIMER

Beijing Encounter

Published by Lonely Planet Publications Pty Ltd
ABN 36 005 607 983

Australia (Head Office)	Locked Bag 1, Footscray, Vic 3011 ☎ 03 8379 8000 fax 03 8379 8111 talk2us@lonelyplanet.com.au
USA	150 Linden St, Oakland, CA 94607 ☎ 510 250 6400 toll free 800 275 8555 fax 510 893 8572 info@lonelyplanet.com
UK	2nd fl, 186 City Rd London EC1V 2NT ☎ 020 7106 2100 fax 020 7106 2101 go@lonelyplanet.co.uk

This edition of *Beijing Encounter* was written by David Eimer. Eilís Quinn wrote the previous edition. This guidebook was commissioned by Lonely Planet's Oakland office and produced by: **Commissioning Editor** Emily K Wolman **Coordinating Editors** Sarah Bailey, Jocelyn Harewood **Coordinating Cartographer** Andras Bogdanovits **Coordinating Layout Designer** Carlos Solarte **Senior Editor** Katie Lynch **Managing Cartographer** David Connolly **Managing Layout Designer** Laura Jane **Assisting Cartographer** Peter Shields **Assisting Layout Designer** Vicki Beale **Cover Research** Dan Baird, lonelyplanetimages.com **Internal Image Research** Sabrina Dalbesio, lonelyplanet images.com **Language Content Coordinator** Annelies Mertens **Project Manager** Chris Love

Thanks to Lucy Birchley, Daniel Corbett, Sally Darmody, Indra Kilfoyle Yvonne Kirk, Rebecca Lalor, Ji Yuanfang

ISBN 978 1 74179 408 3

Printed through Colorcraft Ltd, Hong Kong. Printed in China.

HOW TO USE THIS BOOK
Colour-Coding & Maps

Colour-coding is used for symbols on maps and in the text that they relate to (eg all eating venues on the maps and in the text are given a green knife and fork symbol). Each neighbourhood also gets its own colour, and this is used down the edge of the page and throughout that neighbourhood section.

Shaded yellow areas on the maps denote areas of interest – for their historical significance, their attractive architecture or their great bars and restaurants. We encourage you to head to these areas and just start exploring!

Prices

Multiple prices listed with reviews (eg Y10/5 or Y10/5/20) indicate adult/child, adult/concession or adult/child/family.

Although the authors and Lonely Planet have taken all reasonable care in preparing this book, we make no warranty about the accuracy or completeness of its content and, to the maximum extent permitted, disclaim all liability arising from its use.

DAVID EIMER

David first came to China in 1988, when both Westerners and cars were in short supply. After studying law, he abandoned the idea of becoming a barrister for a career as a freelance journalist. That took him from London to LA for five years, where he wrote for a variety of newspapers and magazines. Back in London, he returned to China for the first time in 14 years and found a country that had changed beyond almost all recognition. Subsequent visits confirmed his belief that China was the most exciting country in the world, and in early 2005 he moved to Beijing and took up residence in a *hutong* in Dongcheng district and contributes to UK and Hong Kong publications. He has co-authored the last two editions of the *Beijing* guide for Lonely Planet and worked on the *Shanghai* and *China* guidebooks.

DAVID'S THANKS

Special gratitude goes to Li Ying for her invaluable assistance and patience. Thanks to Halla Mohieddeen for her crucial insights and to all the people who passed on tips, whether knowingly or unwittingly. Thanks also to Emily Wolman and David Connolly at Lonely Planet.

Thanks to Eilís Quinn for her work on the previous edition.

THE PHOTOGRAPHER

Greg Elms has contributed to Lonely Planet for over 15 years. Armed with a Bachelor of Arts in Photography, Greg was a photographer's assistant before embarking on a travel odyssey until he eventually settled down to a freelance career in Melbourne.

Our readers Many thanks to the travellers who wrote to us with helpful hints, useful advice and interesting anecdotes: Howard Bull, Bob Saltzstein, Dana Schindel, Brooklyn Storme, Emanuela Tasinato.

Cover photograph A woman on her phone – today's China is a well-blended mix of the traditional and the modern, Peter Beck/Corbis. **Internal photographs** by David Eimer p43, p58, p62, p75, p83, p103. All other photographs by Lonely Planet Images and Greg Elms except those by Jinghui Cai p61; Bob Charlton p69; Krzysztof Dydynski p114; Lee Foster p21; John Hay p4; Richard l'Anson p128; Ray Laskowitz p27, p100, p121; Keren Su p119, p132; Phil Weymouth p30 (top), p135; Lawrie Williams p25; Rodney Zandbergs p130.

All images are copyright of the photographers unless otherwise indicated. Many of the images in this guide are available for licensing from **Lonely Planet Images:** lonelyplanetimages.com

Charming Liulichang (p126) – just the street to browse for antiques

CONTENTS

THIS IS BEIJING

Capital of the country everyone's talking about, Beijing is a dynamic clash of the ancient and the modern. Steeped in history it might be, but Beijing redefines and reinvents itself while other cities are content to rest on their laurels.

If the pace of change in Beijing leaves its almost 17 million residents breathless, then visitors to the city are frequently left open-mouthed by its contrasts. Stunning historical sights rub shoulders with cutting-edge architecture, while serene temples coexist with buzzing nightspots. And if that wasn't enough, Beijing is home to Asia's most exciting art scene, as well as upwards of 60,000 restaurants offering the very best of China's many cuisines.

More than anything, though, there's a confidence to Beijing now – a very real sense that this once conservative capital is enjoying the time of its life. Its inhabitants know that better than anyone. Beijingers have always believed they're living at the centre of the world; now, they really are. Always direct and never short of something to say and joke about, the locals are fiercely proud of their city and are no longer fazed or left tongue-tied by the increasing numbers of foreigners who have come to see what all the fuss is about.

Nevertheless, for all the new buildings, the improvements to infrastructure and the dramatic rise in living standards, Beijing remains a work in progress. Pollution is still an issue, no longer caused by heavy industry but by the 1000 new cars that take to the roads every day. And constant change brings its own stresses, as neighbourhoods are overhauled and once familiar landmarks disappear. Many people, too, have failed to prosper from the booming local economy.

But for all its inequalities, Beijing positively seethes with energy and optimism. There's nowhere else on the planet where you can see history being made on this scale, so grab the chance while you can.

Top left Peking Opera performance, Chaoyang Theatre (p64) **Top right** Artworks are on display indoors and out, in the Dashanzi Art District (p16) **Bottom** Every night is a good night at the restaurant strips by the lakes of Houhai (p88)

>HIGHLIGHTS

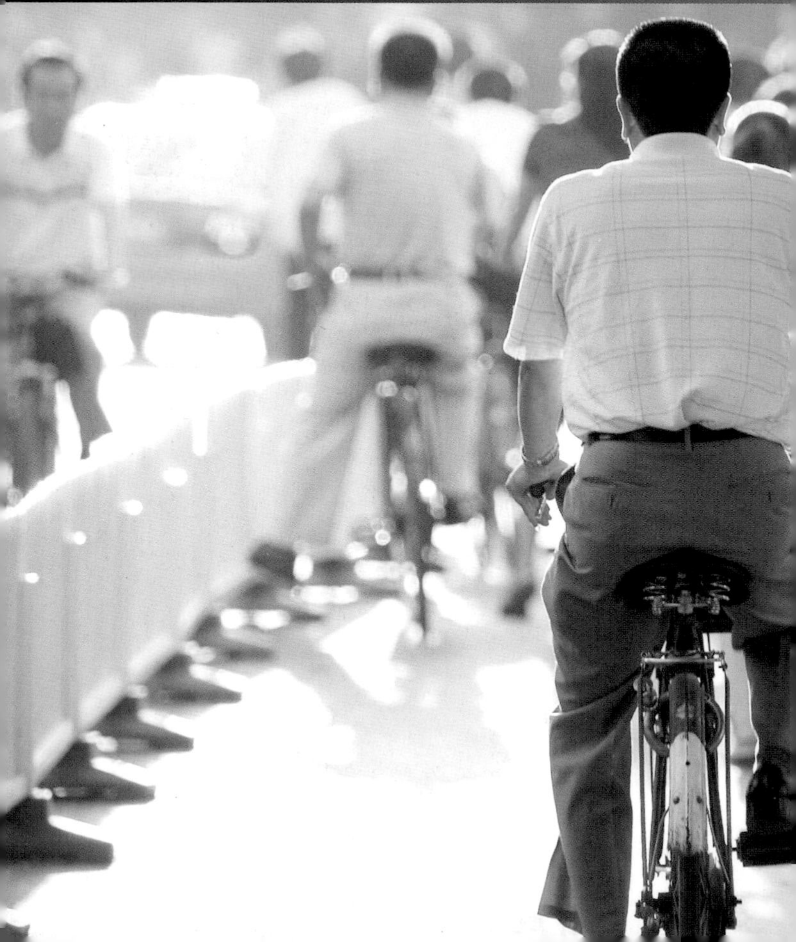

Rush hour in Chaoyang, when cyclists and pedestrians fill the streets (p52)

HIGHLIGHTS

>1 FORBIDDEN CITY 故宫
WALK IN THE FOOTSTEPS OF EMPERORS AT THE FORBIDDEN CITY

Once home to China's emperors, the Forbidden City was the very heart of the country for five centuries and even now exerts a powerful pull on the nation's psyche. So called because an unauthorised visit to the palace would result in instant death, it's the best-preserved collection of ancient architecture in China and is absolutely unmissable.

Originally laid out by Emperor Yongle, with the help of a mere million labourers, between 1406 and 1420, the complex is so vast – 800 buildings with 9000 rooms spread out over 720,000 sq metres – that a full-time restoration squad is continuously repainting and repairing. It's estimated that it would take 10 years to do a full renovation.

Most of the buildings visitors see today, though, date back to the 18th century. Fire was always a threat to the wooden palace and blazes were frequent, with wayward fireworks displays and knocked-over lanterns, as well as the odd angry eunuch, the main culprits. Scattered around the complex are the bronze vats that contained the water kept on hand to put out fires.

But the palace isn't just a collection of buildings. It is actually a huge museum with the largest collection of imperial treasures in the country, including the superb Dragon Throne the emperor sat on and Buddhas bedecked with almost every precious metal and gemstone imaginable. Despite being looted by the Japanese and the Nationalists last century, there are still so many artefacts that only a fraction can be shown at any one time. Most can be found in the pavilions and side buildings that act as mini-museums, with rotating displays of exhibits.

Equally enchanting are the courtyards that separate the buildings. They're fine places to contemplate the splendour of the palace and the life lived by its inhabitants. Fourteen Ming and 10 Qing emperors called the Forbidden City home and the intrigue, scandal and drama that went on here has inspired countless films and books. The imperial family was catered to by vast armies of servants – cooks, concubines, eunuchs, officials and soldiers – who pampered them while also scheming to improve their own positions.

Unsurprisingly, many emperors were insulated by the luxury they lived in and knew little of the dire conditions endured by most ordinary Chinese outside the palace walls. It was that isolation that caused their downfall. For more info, see the boxed text, p44.

>2 TIANANMEN SQUARE
天安门广场

DODGE KITES ON THE WORLD'S BIGGEST URBAN SQUARE

The world's largest public square, Tiananmen Sq was conceived by Mao Zedong as a monument to the omnipotence of the communist party. At 440,000 sq metres, the huge expanse of concrete is certainly awe-inspiring. Most visitors get to know it well, as they criss-cross it on their way to and from the Forbidden City (see the boxed text, p44), Qianmen (p46), the Chairman Mao Memorial Hall (p39) and the Great Hall of the People (p88).

It's at its most evocative at sunrise and sundown, when a crack squad of People's Liberation Army (PLA) soldiers goose-step their way across the square to raise and lower the Chinese flag. At night, it's especially beautiful when the crowds thin out and locals arrive to unfurl high-altitude, glow-in-the-dark kites. But any time, the lack of high-rise buildings in the proximity emphasises the grandeur and scale of the square.

Named for Tiananmen Gate (Gate of Heavenly Peace; pictured right; see also p46), the arched 15th-century gate just to the north, the square has witnessed some of the key moments in Chinese history. Mao proclaimed the People's Republic of China from Tiananmen Gate to a huge crowd of ecstatic Beijingers, and throughout the Mao era the square regularly packed with a million-odd people for parades. In 1989 it was the site of the doomed pro-democracy protests, which ended when tanks rolled across the square.

Seven parallel bridges lead over a stream from the square to Tiananmen Gate's five doors. In pre-revolution days, the centre

TIANANMEN FLAG CEREMONY

Tiananmen Sq's flag is lowered every evening at sunset. The soldiers are drilled to march at 108 paces per minute, 75cm per pace. It's so precisely timed that the flag disappears underneath Tiananmen Gate at exactly the same second that the sun disappears. The same thing happens in reverse at sunrise, except with a scratchy recording of the Chinese national anthem playing in the background.

bridge and door could only be used by the emperor. Since the arrival of the communists, this door has been crowned with an enormous portrait of Mao, an obligatory photo opportunity for the domestic tourists who swarm over the square every day.

As well as tour groups, kite fliers and a small army of hawkers, Tiananmen is populated by numerous police, PLA and plain-clothes officers, ready to pounce at any sign of a protest. Their presence is a re-minder that the square is not like public places elsewhere in the world, despite the kids running around and the tourists snapping away.

>3 SUMMER PALACE 圆明园

ESCAPE THE HEAT AT THE ROYALS' SUMMER PLAYGROUND

A stunning collection of beautifully landscaped pavilions, temples, gardens, corridors and bridges set around the tranquil Kunming Lake, the Summer Palace was where the royal court came to escape the heat and humidity of Beijing's summer. Nowadays, tour groups do the same and the palace is especially busy on weekends and national holidays. But during the week it can be an idyllic spot, and it's easy to see why some emperors chose to spend as much time here as they could.

The area had been a royal garden, before Emperor Qianlong (1711–99) set about turning it into a retreat fit for the son of heaven. A team of 100,000 labourers was enlisted to build everything the imperial family might need for its summer hols, including a theatre for Peking opera and temples on Longevity Hill featuring everything from Chinese Confucian symbols to Tibetan Buddhist features.

At the same time, Kunming Lake was enlarged so that the emperor could personally supervise naval drills. Visitors today can cruise

the lake before arriving at its northern shore, where the spectacular, intricately painted Long Corridor leads to Longevity Hill, which you can climb for a view over distant Beijing.

Although the complex was off-limits to foreigners for much of the Qing dynasty, Anglo-French troops stormed it in 1860 during the Second Opium War and did much damage. Empress Cixi restored it, but foreign soldiers returned in 1900 in the aftermath of the Boxer Rebellion and trashed it once more. The palace was never the same again and fell into serious disrepair after the fall of the Qing. It was only after the communists took power that restoration work began. See the boxed text, p95, for further details.

WALKING THE WESTERN CORRIDOR

The Western Corridor (Map p95) is possibly the most beautiful part of the Summer Palace. An artificial spit of land, it's as narrow as 4m in many places, strung with precariously arched stone bridges and lined on both sides by weeping willows. This is where locals hang out when they visit, and no matter how many tour groups flood the imperial residences or temples, walking the Western Corridor will give you a peaceful and unique peek into a little-visited part of the palace.

>4 798 ART DISTRICT/DASHANZI
大山子艺术区

SNAP UP THE NEXT BIG THING AT THE GALLERIES OF THE 798 ART DISTRICT

A disused electronics factory might seem like a strange home for Asia's most vibrant contemporary art scene, but the 798 Art District in Dashanzi is testament to the creativity and ingenuity of China's artists. Built in the 1950s with East German architectural and industrial know-how, the sprawling factory was taken over in the late 1990s by artists, who found its vast spaces perfect for studios and galleries. Now it's one of the most talked-about destinations in Beijing.

The market for Chinese contemporary art might not be as red-hot as it was a couple of years ago, when prices soared and artists such as Yue Minjun and Ai Weiwei were some of the most sought after in the world. But more and more cashed-up Beijingers are buying, and 798 continues to thrive, with hundreds of emerging artists waiting to be discovered.

Spending the day trawling the galleries is great fun. The area is one of the most cosmopolitan in Beijing and attracts hipsters, artists, serious collectors and art lovers, drawn as much by the cafes and boutiques that have sprung up alongside the galleries as by the galleries themselves. If you're interested in buying, it pays to do some research first. Above all, buy what appeals to you, not what you think will increase in price. See the boxed text, p56.

>5 HUTONG 胡同

LOSE YOURSELF IN THE CITY'S ANCIENT ALLEYWAYS

Criss-crossing the centre of Beijing, the *hutong* (alleyways) are the very soul of the capital. To pass through these ancient streets (dating back 900 years in some cases) is to step back in time to old Beijing. They're also by far the best places to experience Beijing street life in all its glory. Still home to tens of thousands of locals, they teem with people working, eating, drinking, playing mah jong and Chinese chess, or just watching the world go by.

At one time, 6000 of these enchanting alleyways were dotted throughout Beijing. The smartest could be found close to the Forbidden City (see the boxed text, p44), where large *siheyuan* (courtyard houses) were home to the Beijing elite. But from the 1980s, as Beijing began modernising, many *hutong* fell victim to the wrecking ball.

Beijing's government is now aware of both the historical value of the *hutong* and their tourism potential, and have belatedly protected some by law. Others, like Nanluogu Xiang (Map pp40–1, B3), have become nightlife hotspots. Most *hutong* are in Chongwen (p66), Dongcheng (pictured above; p38), Xicheng (p86) and Xuanwu (p80).

By far the best way to experience the *hutong* is to explore them on foot or by bike. If you prefer, rickshaw-driver tours are plentiful around Qianhai Lake (Map p87, D3). Don't worry about finding the drivers; they'll find you. The China Culture Center (p149) also offers tours.

>6 TEMPLE OF HEAVEN 天坛公园

MARVEL AT THIS ULTIMATE EXPRESSION OF MING DYNASTY ARCHITECTURE

A cosmological marvel and loaded with enough symbolism to keep any amateur necromancer busy for years, the Temple of Heaven is unlike any other temple in Beijing, or anywhere else for that matter. Every part of this utterly unique complex of halls is there for a reason. The temple is the ultimate expression of Ming dynasty architecture.

Set inside a walled 267-hectare park, the temple (known to Beijingers as Tiantan) was where China's emperors came to pray for divine guidance and good harvests and to atone for the sins of the people. As such, the complex was built to be viewed by the gods. Seen from above, the temples are round and their bases square, a pattern based on the ancient Chinese belief that heaven is round and earth is square. The shape of the park also reflects this, with the northern end a semicircle and the southern end a square.

The Hall of Prayer for Good Harvests is the temple's star attraction. Its ornate roof is decorated in stunning blue, yellow and green glazed tiles, representing heaven, earth and the mortal world. Inside the hall, immense pillars symbolise the four seasons and the 12 months of the year. Burnt down by a lightning strike in 1889 – a seriously bad omen for the already struggling Qing dynasty – the hall was rebuilt the next year with fir trees shipped from Oregon. Amazingly, the whole structure holds together without nails or cement.

South of here, the octagonal Imperial Vault (shaped like a mini-version of the Hall of Prayer for Good Harvests) held tablets belonging to the emperor's ancestors to be used during the winter solstice ceremony, the most important ritual of the year. Surrounding the vault is the Echo Wall, said to be such a perfect semicircle that a whisper at one end can be carried around to the other side.

Leading up to the vault are the Triple Sounds Stones. If you stand here and clap your hands, the echo should come back once from the first stone, twice from the second and thrice from the third, although it can be hard to test this out as dozens of other people will be right next to you trying to do exactly the same thing. Just south is the Round Altar, where the emperor performed his rituals; the stones,

stairs and columns here are arranged in groups or multiples of nine, which was considered a heavenly number.

As well as its historical significance, Tiantan is also a working park and one of the most pleasant in Beijing. Ancient cypress trees are dotted throughout and it's popular with the city's senior citizens. Get here soon after dawn, before the temple structures are open, and you'll find them dancing to sedate ballroom music and practising taichi. See also p69.

>7 MODERN ARCHITECTURE

CHECK OUT BEIJING'S CHANGING SKYLINE

Ten years ago Beijing was a city in thrall to Stalinist-inspired architecture. How things have changed. Now the world's leading architects head for the Chinese capital, as some of the most eye-catching and controversial structures built anywhere transform Beijing's skyline.

The 2008 Olympics was the catalyst for Beijing to embrace the avant-garde. The Bird's Nest Olympic Stadium, an intricate web of steel girders, was a stunning centrepiece for the games, while many visitors to Beijing take their first steps on Chinese soil in Beijing airport's vast Norman Foster–designed Terminal 3 building with its dragon-like roof.

But other buildings, too, signal Beijing's ambition to become a true world city. The new headquarters of CCTV (p74), China's state broadcaster, is perhaps the most awesome of them all. Designed by Rem Koolhaus, it's a jaw-dropping continuous loop of a building that looms over the CBD. Meanwhile, the Cui Kai–designed Capital Museum (p88) has finally given Beijing a modern museum befitting the city's status.

Not all the new architecture has been welcomed by Beijingers. The National Centre for the Performing Arts (pictured above; p91), sometimes known as the National Grand Theatre, has attracted much scorn. Designed by Paul Andreu, it has some remarkable features, but for many locals its dome-like structure is inappropriate for its location close to the Forbidden City; it has become known as the 'alien egg'.

>8 PEKING DUCK 北京烤鸭

FEAST ON BEIJING'S SIGNATURE DISH

Its fame has spread around the world, but nothing beats tucking into Beijing's most iconic dish in the city where it originated. Peking duck was an imperial delicacy as far back as the Yuan dynasty (1206–1368), but it wasn't until the fall of the Qing dynasty in 1911 that ordinary people got to sample its delights, as newly unemployed royal chefs set up restaurants around Beijing.

Reared on special farms outside the capital, the ducks go through a lengthy preparation process before reaching the dinner table. First, the (dead) bird is inflated by blowing air between its skin and body. The skin is then pricked and the duck is doused in boiling water. Finally, it's hung up to air dry before being roasted. When cooked, the duck's skin is crispy on the outside and the meat is juicy on the inside. The bird is then meticulously sliced and served with sauce, pancakes, green onions and cucumber.

These days there are all sorts of variations on the original recipe and a huge array of restaurants that serve it. See the boxed text, p123, for a list of the best places.

>9 PANJIAYUAN ANTIQUE MARKET
潘家园古玩市场

HIT BEIJING'S MOST FAMOUS FLEA MARKET BEFORE DAWN

Every weekend up to 50,000 bargain hunters head to Panjiayuan for the most colourful shopping spectacle in Beijing. But it's a good idea to get there before the sun comes up, when it will be just you, the 3000-odd stallholders and dozens of flashlight-wielding antique aficionados. Watching these collectors scour the huge market for that Ming vase or Qing-era sculpture that nobody has noticed is a sight in itself. The haggling here is hard-core too, and not for the faint-hearted.

Panjiayuan started life in 1980 as a humble, and illegal, *hutong* market for Beijingers looking to raise cash by selling off their family heirlooms. By 1990 it was so popular it had relocated to its present site. And after several well-publicised finds early on, it has attracted both local and foreign visitors in huge numbers.

These days, though, the chances of stumbling across a priceless treasure are remote, unless you're standing in line with the antique dealers for the 4.30am opening on Saturday. But the market is still home to an extraordinary A-Z of Middle Kingdom knick-knacks, with everything from Buddhas and Cultural Revolution–era memorabilia to military gear and Tibetan carpets. See p76.

>10 PEKING OPERA 京剧

GET A FRONT-ROW SEAT AT BEIJING'S OLDEST ART FORM

With its madcap mix of piercing songs, elaborate costumes and make-up and low comedy, Peking opera can seem utterly alien to most foreigners. But it's well worth experiencing, because this 900-year-old art form is China's contribution to world theatre, as well as being a unique blend of martial arts, stylised dance and poetic arias.

Traditionally, only men could be performers, and they were at the very bottom of the social ladder, on a par with prostitutes and slaves. With most shows held outside, the actors developed a shrill style of singing that could be heard above the crowds, and they wore garish costumes that could be seen through the poor lighting of oil lamps.

Performances continue to be loud and bright, with singers taking on stylised parts instantly recognised by Peking opera fans. The four major roles are the female, the male, the 'painted-face' (for gods and warriors) and the clown. Plot lines are simple and not dissimilar to Shakespearean tragedy, with plenty of comic relief. Above all, Peking opera is as much a visual experience as a musical one.

There's an excellent range of places to watch Peking opera in Beijing, including the historic Huguang Guild Hall (p84) and the Lao She Tea House (p85). You can also visit the Mei Lanfang Former Residence (p89), a shrine to China's most famous Peking opera performer of all.

>11 ACROBATICS 杂技

WONDER JUST HOW THE PERFORMERS DID THAT AT AN ACROBATICS SHOW

For 2000 years China's acrobats have been wowing audiences with barely feasible displays of daring, while contorting themselves into all sorts of extraordinary shapes. Watching them tumble, balance on high poles or walk tightropes is one of the best tickets in town. Best of all, you don't need to know any Chinese to understand what's going on.

Most of the acts in today's shows are credited to Zhang Heng (AD 25–120), who is believed to have invented such staples as fire breathing, knife swallowing and pole balancing. Hebei province, close to Beijing, was the original bastion of acrobatics, but nowadays youngsters from all over China start training when barely out of the cradle in the hope of graduating to the troupes that tour the world.

There are daily performances at Chaoyang Theatre (pictured above; p64), but a more atmospheric and less touristy venue is Tianqiao Acrobatics Theatre (p85), where the audience is closer to the stage.

>BEIJING DIARY

Beijing becomes a more relaxed city when it erupts in the colour and excitement of its traditional festivals. The roads are less busy as workplaces shut down and the locals take the opportunity to let loose with family and friends. Meanwhile, domestic tourists flood sights to capacity and hotel room rates go up. The dates of many traditional festivals are based on the lunar calendar, so they take place at different times each year. But as well as its age-old celebrations, Beijing hosts an increasing array of arts and music festivals. The dates and locations of these sometimes shift, so check the websites before you arrive.

Worshippers' incense fills the Confucius Temple (p42) with heavenly aromas

JANUARY & FEBRUARY

Spring Festival

Also known as the Chinese New Year, the Spring Festival usually falls in late January or early February and is by far the most important of all China's holidays. At midnight, Beijing's sky explodes in a dazzling display of fireworks that is the cue for family reunions and non-stop firecracker action. Everyone gets a week off work, so people flock to the temple fairs held around town; one of the best fairs to experience is the one at the Lama Temple (p42).

Lantern Festival

Fifteen days after the start of the Spring Festival, lanterns go up in Beijing's major parks, marking the official end of Chinese New Year festivities as well as the first full moon of the new year. Sweet rice dumplings *(yuanxiao)* are traditionally eaten on this day.

MARCH, APRIL & MAY

Birth of Guanyin

A good time to visit Beijing's many temples, the 19th day of the second lunar month is the birthday of Guanyin, the Buddhist Goddess of Mercy; images of her can be found in most Buddhist and Taoist temples.

Tomb Sweeping Day

Now an official public holiday, this is the day the Chinese honour their ancestors. Families visit and clean their relatives' graves and burn paper money in honour of the deceased every 5 April (4 April in leap years).

International Labour Day

Held on 1 May, this day marks the beginning of an official three-day holiday, although many Chinese head off for a week's break. Because of that, tourist sites and transport are choked to capacity at this time.

MUSIC, ART & LITERARY FESTIVALS TO KEEP AN EYE ON

International Literary Festival (www.beijingbookworm.com) For two weeks in March, writers and bibliophiles from China and abroad converge on the Bookworm (p61) for one of the most popular cultural events of the year.

Beijing Ninegates Jazz Festival (www.ninegate.com.cn) Local and international jazz acts are performed over two weeks in May or June.

Beijing Music Festival (www.bmf.org.cn) Held in October, this classical-music festival brings in foreign orchestras and musicians for a month of concerts around town.

Beijing Biennale (www.namoc.org, in Chinese) Staged at Beijing's National Art Museum of China (p42) in odd-numbered years, this art showcase features both Chinese and foreign artists. It's normally held in September or October.

Colourful and shapely – it's traditional to hang lanterns at Chinese festivals

JUNE, JULY & AUGUST

International Children's Day
Every 1 June is devoted to the kids, with under-14s getting a day off school. Expect queues at fast-food restaurants to be longer than usual, as parents treat their children.

Dragon Boat Festival
Beijing's lack of water makes it difficult for the capital to celebrate this festival in the same style as in places like Hong Kong, although reservoirs in the far suburbs sometimes host dragon boat races. But you will see people eating *zongzi* (delicious sticky rice with meat or vegie fillings wrapped in a bamboo leaf). Held on the fifth day of the fifth lunar month (usually in June), the festival honours the ancient poet and official Qu Yuan.

Anniversary of Founding of CCP
No one gets a day off, but the founding of the Chinese Communist Party is celebrated on 1 July with plenty of enthusiastic flag waving at Tiananmen Sq.

Anniversary of Founding of PLA
There's more official flag waving at Tiananmen Sq on 1 August to mark the founding of the People's Liberation Army.

SEPTEMBER, OCTOBER & NOVEMBER

Mid-Autumn Festival

Also known as the Moon Festival and taking place on the 15th or 18th day of the eighth lunar month (usually in September), at the mid-autumn festival families get together to eat moon cakes (*yuebing;* red-bean paste wrapped in pastry).

National Day

On 1 October 1949 Mao proclaimed the establishment of the People's Republic of China from Tiananmen Gate, and each year this day is the start of a week-long holiday. Every decade the day is marked by a massive display of China's military might on Tiananmen Sq.

Confucius' Birthday

The great philosopher's birthday is celebrated with a ceremony at Confucius Temple (p42) on 27 October.

>ITINERARIES

There's romance in the air, on the lakes at Houhai (p88)

ITINERARIES

Maximising your time in a city the size of Beijing is essential. There's so much to see and do that it's easy to miss that sight, market or restaurant you intended to visit. The itineraries below will help you tailor your trip, so you get the most out of this amazing city.

DAY ONE

Make an early start to catch the flag-raising ceremony at Tiananmen Sq (see the boxed text, p12). Then, after buying breakfast from one of the nearby street food vendors, be first in line when the Forbidden City (see the boxed text, p44) opens at 8.30am. Take your time to check out the palace's more far-flung areas, and try to take in one of its little-visited exhibitions of imperial treasures. Exit by the north gate and climb up the hill at Jingshan Park (p88) for superb views of the palace rooftops. From there, walk north through Beihai Park (p88) to Houhai (see the boxed text, p88), where you can eat lakeside at the Han Cang restaurant (p90). Finish the night with a drink at one of the atmospheric bars surrounding the lake.

DAY TWO

Either take a day trip out to the Great Wall (p107) or Chuandixia (p113), or get to know the contemporary side of Beijing. Start with a stroll down Wangfujing Dajie (Map pp40–1, C5), Beijing's premier shopping strip. Then hop the subway to Sanlitun (Map pp54–5, D3) for lunch in one of the international restaurants in the area, like Element Fresh (p57) or Mosto (p59). When your appetite is sated, jump in a cab to the 798 Art District/Dashanzi (see the boxed text, p53), where you can spend the afternoon checking out the galleries and cafes. In the evening, take in a Peking opera performance (p23) or an acrobatics show (p24).

DAY THREE

If day three falls on a Saturday or Sunday, head to the Panjiayuan Antique Market (p76) at dawn and try to outwit the antique dealers. Otherwise, head up to Haidian (p92) to spend the morning roaming the Summer

Top Don't leave without a jacket from the Silk Market (p76) **Bottom** The World of Suzie Wong (p65) is famous for its cocktails

Palace (see the boxed text, p95). After lunch at one of Wudaokou's Korean restaurants (p102), make your way to the humming *hutong* (alleyway) of Nanluogu Xiang (Map pp40–1, B3) and explore the surrounding alleyways. Once night falls, it's time for Peking duck at Beijing Dadong Roast Duck Restaurant (p49) or Liqun Roast Duck Restaurant (p71), before heading to LAN (p78) to mingle with Beijing's beautiful people. Alternatively, catch a show at the controversial National Centre for the Performing Arts (p91).

BLISSFUL BEIJING

If haggling at the markets has taken its toll, or if you're drained from navigating your way through the Forbidden City's crowds, take a day out to recharge, Beijing-style. Roll out of bed at 6am to try taichi with the senior citizens at the Temple of Heaven Park (p69). Then once your *qi* (energy) is centred, treat yourself to one of Beijing's famous body or foot massages at Dragonfly (p51).

RAINY DAYS

When it rains in Beijing, it comes down in sheets. The excellent Capital Museum (p88) is a great place to stay dry while you wait it out and has so many exhibits you could spend the whole day there without even knowing it. Rainy days are also the perfect time to hole up in the Bookworm (p61), which has over 16,000 books, as well as wi-fi and food and drink, to keep you amused.

FORWARD PLANNING

Three weeks before you go Book your hotel room, check whether your visit coincides with any major festivals (p25), and start scanning Beijing-related websites (p149) to find out what's going on in the city. Make sure your visa is in order. Buy yourself a Mandarin phrasebook.

One week before you go If you're going to Beijing for work, get some business cards printed. Research possible day trips and start reading *The Beijinger* (www.thebeijinger.com) for the latest news on upcoming cultural events and the hottest restaurants, bars and clubs. Rent a Beijing-set DVD, like *The Last Emperor* or *Lost in Beijing*.

The day before you go Reconfirm your flight; print out the address of your hotel in Chinese to give to the taxi driver when you get to the airport; pack your phrasebook; and, most importantly, make a dinner reservation at one of Beijing's most popular restaurants, such as Salt (p60) or Maison Boulud (p50).

FOR FREE

If you want to give your wallet or purse a break, you won't be bored in Beijing. Though it doesn't have the kind of 'free' or 'discount' museum days some other cities have, Beijing makes up for that with its fascinating street life. You could spend days wandering the *hutong* of Dongcheng (p38) where you'll see how ordinary Beijingers live. Markets like the Silk Market (p76) are also great places to experience the cut and thrust of Beijing life. Alternatively, green spaces like Ritan Park (p74) are good places to while away a few hours. Head to the former sun altar and see if anyone will let you join their kung fu lesson for free.

>DISTRICTS

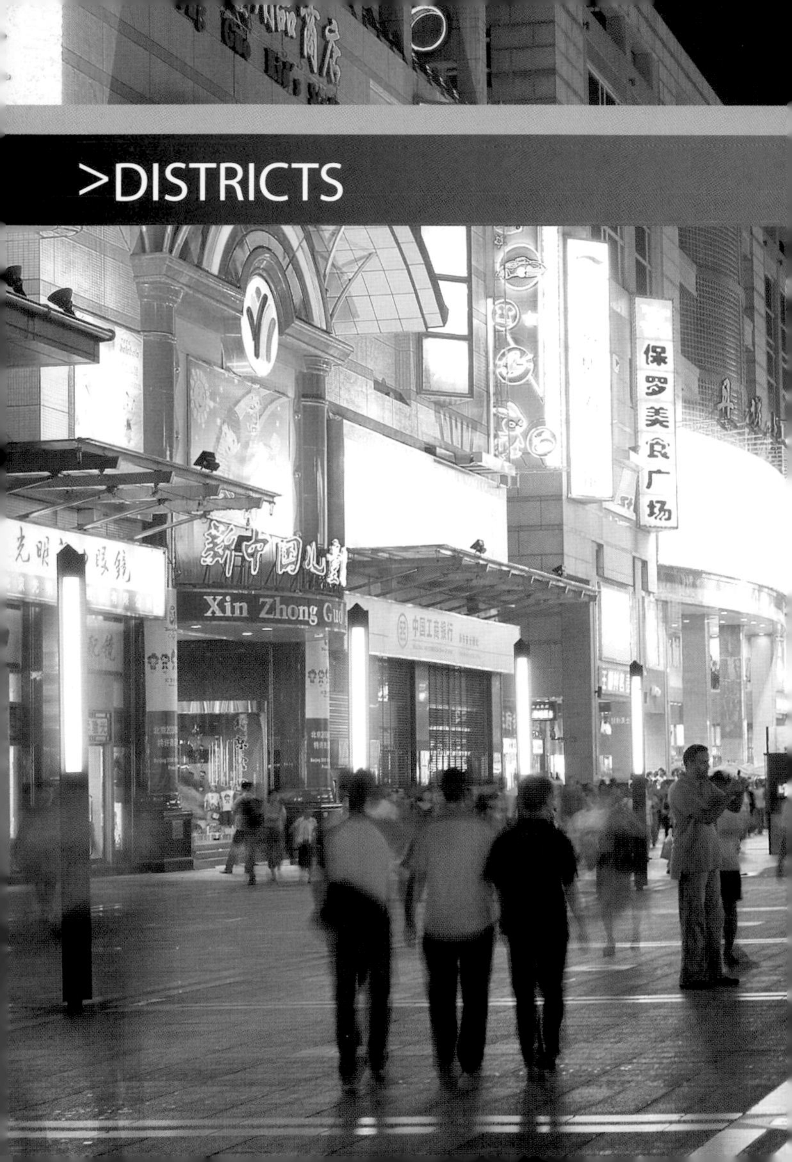

A night stroll on pedestrianised Wangfujing Dajie, Dongcheng (p126)

DISTRICTS

Beijing's six main districts are a dazzling mix of the new and the old. Just remember to keep your eyes open, or you'll miss something.

Dongcheng lies at the heart of the city and is where many of Beijing's iconic sights can be found. The district is home to Tiananmen Sq and the Forbidden City, as well as Beijing's best-preserved and most extensive *hutong* (alleyways). There's also a great selection of restaurants, a decent range of accommodation and Beijing's most famous shopping street, Wangfujing Dajie.

To the east and northeast of Dongcheng lies the vast Chaoyang district, which we've divided into north and south Chaoyang. North Chaoyang is Beijing's nightlife hub, with many of the most happening bars and clubs. Housing many of the city's embassies, it also has several of Beijing's best international restaurants and hotels. South Chaoyang is a shopper's delight, with some of the city's best-known markets, while the booming central business district features an increasing number of up-scale bars and restaurants.

Head to Chongwen, southeast of the city centre, for fantastic Ming dynasty–era sights, including the spectacular Temple of Heaven and the remains of Beijing's once mighty city walls. Go too for fine Peking duck restaurants. To the west, Chongwen's neighbour Xuanwu has atmospheric *hutong* and shopping streets that date back hundreds of years.

North of here, Xicheng has been transformed by some of Beijing's most daring new buildings, including the Capital Museum and the National Centre for the Performing Arts. The Houhai Lake area has thriving restaurants and nightlife and is a favourite destination for the locals.

Haidian dominates much of northwest Beijing and is where you'll find the city's most prestigious universities and biggest parks. The district's Wudaokou neighbourhood has a buzzing, student-driven music scene, along with fine Korean and Japanese restaurants.

Beijing's nine-line subway system is much more comprehensive than it once was and you'll be able to get almost everywhere using it. Several more lines are currently being built.

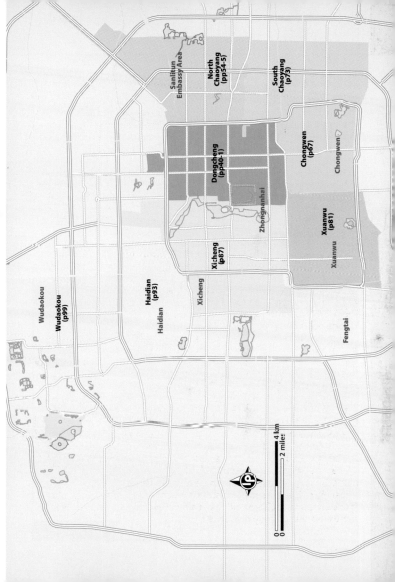

Sanlitun
Embassy Area

North
Chaoyang
(pp54-5)

South
Chaoyang
(p73)

Dongcheng
(pp40-1)

Chongwen
(p67)

Chongwen

Zhongnanhai

Xicheng
(p87)

Xuanwu
(p81)

Xicheng

Xuanwu

Wudaokou

Wudaokou
(p99)

Haidian
(p93)

Haidian

Fengtai

0   4 km

0   2 miles

DISTRICTS

DONGCHENG

>DONGCHENG 东城

With blockbuster sights like the Forbidden City and Tiananmen Sq, thriving *hutong* (alleyways), some fantastic restaurants and bars, and the showy shopping street Wangfujing Dajie, Dongcheng is the most exciting and varied district in Beijing. It's a great place for visitors to be based.

Most of the principal sights are concentrated in the south of Dongcheng, where you'll also find pedestrian-only Wangfujing Dajie with its department stores and the famous Donghuamen Night Market, with its selection of exotic street food. Dongcheng's north has the most lively *hutong* in town, including the nightlife and shopping hub of Nanluogu Xiang and the area around the historic Drum and Bell Towers.

Zipping around Dongcheng is easy, thanks to the presence of lines 2 and 5 of the subway, which can get you from the south of the district to the north in 10 minutes. Dongcheng is also the best district in Beijing to get around on two wheels.

DONGCHENG

◎ SEE
Beijing Imperial City
  Art Museum **1** B7
Beijing Police Museum ..**2** B8
Bell Tower **3** B3
Chairman Mao
  Memorial Hall **4** B8
Confucius Temple &
  Imperial College **5** D2
Ditan Park **6** C1
Drum Tower **7** B3
Forbidden City **8** B6
Lama Temple **9** D2
National Art
  Museum of China **10** C5
Poly Art Museum **11** E4
Qianmen **12** B8
Tiananmen Gate (Gate
  of Heavenly Peace) ..**13** B7
Workers' Cultural
  Palace **14** B7

⌂ SHOP
Bannerman Tang's
  Toys & Crafts **15** C2
Foreign Languages
  Bookstore **16** C6
Grifted **17** B3
Lu Ping
  Trendsetters **18** B3
Plastered T-Shirts **19** B3
Ten Fu's Tea **20** C7
Zhaoyuange **21** C7

▥ EAT
Baguo Buyi **22** B4
Baihe Vegetarian
  Restaurant **23** E3
Beijing Dadong Roast
  Duck Restaurant **24** E4
Dali Courtyard **25** C3
Ding Ding Xiang **26** F4

Donghuamen
  Night Market **27** C6
Hua Jia Yi Yuan **28** D3
Maison Boulud **29** B8
Source **30** C4
Vineyard Café **31** D2

▣ DRINK
Drum & Bell **32** B3
Passby Bar **33** B3
Yin **34** B6

★ PLAY
Dragonfly Therapeutic
  Retreat **35** B6
Yugong Yishan **36** D4

Please see over for map

👁 SEE

🟢 BEIJING IMPERIAL CITY ART MUSEUM 皇城艺术馆

☎ 8511 5114; 9 Changpu Heyan 菖蒲河沿9号; admission Y20; ⏱ 10am-5.30pm, last entry 4.30pm; Ⓜ Tiananmen Dong

Devoted to maintaining the memory of the imperial city, this museum has visitor-friendly English captions, a permanent collection of impressive Ming- and Qing-era ornaments and rotating temporary exhibits, often from the Forbidden City. Check out the diorama of old Beijing for a sense of how impressive the imperial city was.

🟢 BEIJING POLICE MUSEUM 北京警察博物馆

☎ 8522 5018; 36 Dongjiaomin Xiang 东交民巷36号; admission Y5; ⏱ 9am-4pm Tue-Sun; Ⓜ Qianmen

A fascinating insight into the Beijing underworld and the police you see everywhere in the city. There are plenty of English captions and details of crackdowns on brothels, class traitors, opium dens and spies, as well as uniforms, weapons and gruesome crime-scene photos.

🟢 BELL TOWER 钟楼

9 Zhonglouwan Hutong 钟楼湾胡同9号; admission Y15; ⏱ 9am-5pm; Ⓜ Gulou Dajie

First constructed in 1272 but felled numerous times by fire, the tower's present structure dates from 1745. Climb up the steep steps (carefully) to gawk at the 63-tonne bell. The Drum Tower (p42) is just south.

🟢 CHAIRMAN MAO MEMORIAL HALL 毛主席纪念堂

☎ 6513 2277; Tiananmen Sq 天安门广场; admission free; ⏱ 8.30-noon Tue-Sun, 2-4pm Tue & Thu, mornings only Jul & Aug; Ⓜ Qianmen

One of the few freebies in Beijing is the chance to see the pickled body of the Great Helmsman. Reverent domestic tourists file past in their droves, so no snickering. Occasional mummy maintenance means Mao's body isn't always here. The compulsory bag check (up to Y10) is across the street. See also p12.

The Bell Tower – built before alarm clocks

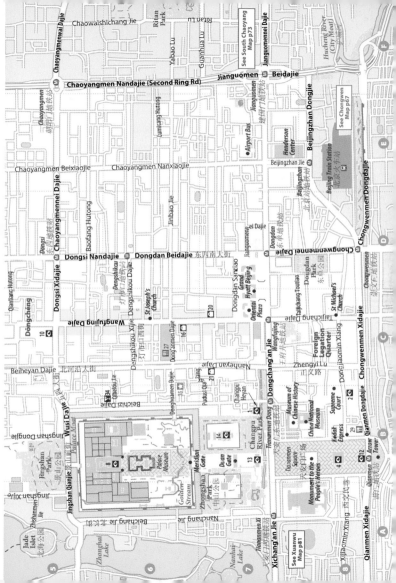

CONFUCIUS TEMPLE & IMPERIAL COLLEGE
孔庙与国子监

☎ 8401 1977; 13 Guozljian Jie; 国子监13号; admission Y20; ⏲ 8.30am-5pm, last entry 4.30pm; Ⓜ Yonghegong-Lama Temple

China's second-largest Confucian temple was recently restored to its former glory and is now a super sanctuary from the chaos and noise of Beijing's streets. Next door, connected by a path, is the former Imperial College, where emperors presented Confucian classics to rapt audiences of students and scholars.

DITAN PARK 地坛公园

☎ 6421 4657; Andingmen Dongdajie 安定门东大街; admission Y2; ⏲ 6am-9pm; Ⓜ Yonghegong-Lama Temple

Imperial rulers once made offerings to the Earth God from Ditan's square-shaped altar. Nowadays, local residents flood into the park for their daily gossip or to power walk along the shady lanes. An excellent temple fair takes place here during the Spring Festival (see p26).

DRUM TOWER 鼓楼

Gulou Dongdajie 鼓楼东大街; admission Y20; ⏲ 9am-5pm; Ⓜ Gulou Dajie

Dominating the area, the drum tower provides a great view over the nearby *hutong* rooftops. The

drums were beaten here hourly in ancient times to keep the proles punctual. The Bell Tower (p39) is just to the north.

LAMA TEMPLE 雍和宫

☎ 6404 4499; 28 Yonghegong Dajie 雍和宫大街28号; admission Y25; ⏲ 9am-4.30pm; Ⓜ Yonghegong-Lama Temple

Ornately decorated, the Lama Temple is one of Beijing's most popular places of worship. Emperor Yongzheng once lived here; now it is home to mostly Mongolian monks who follow the Yellow Hat sect of Tibetan Buddhism. Don't miss Wanfu Pavilion, the final hall, which contains an 18m-high statue of the Maitreya Buddha, supposedly sculpted from a single block of sandalwood. An audio-guide to the pavilion is Y20.

NATIONAL ART MUSEUM OF CHINA 中国美术馆

☎ 6401 7076; www.namoc.org, in Chinese; 1 Wusi Dajie 五四大街1号; admission Y20; ⏲ 9am-4pm Tue-Sun; Ⓜ Dongsi

More English captions would be nice, but this professional museum attracts Chinese art lovers with often excellent temporary exhibitions of modern and contemporary art from home and abroad.

Guan Yichang

This 69-year-old retired school teacher was born and has lived in the hutong near the Drum Tower all his life

What were the *hutong* like when you were a kid? None of the courtyard houses had been divided up; that happened after the Cultural Revolution. My family shared a large courtyard in Xiang Er Hutong with two other families. No one was rich but no one was starving, so I suppose we were middle-class. **Beijing must have been a very different city then.** It was still the old town. The city walls hadn't been knocked down and the people living in the *hutong* were real old Beijingers, the ones who've been here since the late Ming dynasty, like my family. **What changes to Beijing do you notice the most?** Living conditions are much better. But there was much more of a community before they started demolishing a lot of the *hutong*. **Wouldn't you prefer to live in a modern apartment?** Even if I had the money to buy an apartment, I'd still want to live in the *hutong*. Living here, you're in touch with the earth. In an apartment block, you're too far from the ground.

FORBIDDEN CITY 紫禁城

For 500 years commoners were prohibited from entering the **Forbidden City** (☎ 6513 2255; www.dpm.org.cn; Dongchang'an Jie 东长安街; admission Nov-Mar Y40, Apr Oct Y60; ⏰ 8.30am-4pm May-Sep, 8.30am-3.30pm Oct-Apr; 🚇 Tiananmen Xi or Tiananmen Dong). Now, anyone willing to pay the entrance fee can experience this extraordinary palace.

The Forbidden City was initially built under the auspices of Emperor Yongle between 1406 and 1420. From then until the fall of the Qing dynasty in 1911, this sprawling complex was the seat of Chinese government.

Despite its venerable age, the combination of wooden architecture and naked flame (lantern festivals, fireworks, arson) has meant that parts of the palace have been incinerated and rebuilt many times over the centuries. Consequently, much of the present-day Forbidden City dates from the 18th century onwards.

Despite the fact that only around half the complex is open to visitors, it's still so vast that you could easily spend several days exploring it. One possible itinerary is to begin your tour at the **Three Great Halls**, the heart of the palace. Start with the **Hall of Supreme Harmony**, the palace's biggest and most important structure. This was the site of the imperial court's grandest events, including coronations and royal birthdays. Inside the hall, the throne is guarded by two *luduan* (mythical beasts who can detect if a person is lying).

North of here, the **Hall of Middle Harmony** was a kind of backstage area where the emperor stopped to compose himself and consult with ministers before entering the Hall of Supreme Harmony. Next, the **Hall of Preserving Harmony** was used for state banquets and later for imperial examinations. Behind the hall, a 17m marble carriageway carved with dragons leads up to the entrance.

The royals' former living quarters are at the back of the palace grounds. The emperor resided in the **Palace of Heavenly Purity**, until the mid-Qing dynasty when it became an audience hall in which ambassadors and other luminaries were received. The empress's digs were in the **Palace of Earthly Tranquillity**.

On the western and eastern sides of the Forbidden City are an assortment of libraries, temples, theatres and gardens. Some are now museums that require additional entry fees. Make sure you visit the **Hall of Jewellery** (admission Y10), and don't miss the **Clocks & Watches Gallery** (admission Y10). The gallery boasts a dazzling array of timepieces, many of which were gifts to the Qing emperors from abroad.

At the northern end of the Forbidden City is the **Imperial Garden**, a classical Chinese garden with 7000 sq metres of fine landscaping, including rockeries, walkways, pavilions and ancient – carbuncular and deformed – cypresses.

An audio-guide is available for Y40, with a Y100 deposit. For more background on the Forbidden City, see p10.

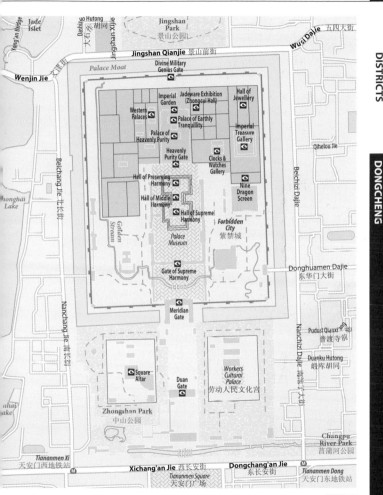

⊙ POLY ART MUSEUM
保利艺术博物馆
☎ 6500 8117; www.polyculture.com
.cn; New Poly Plaza, Chaoyangmen
Beidajie 新保利大厦, 朝阳门北大
街; admission Y20; ⏰ 9.30am-4.30pm;
Ⓜ Dongsishitiao
An arm of the government, the
Poly Group set up this museum
to house the incredible bronzes
and stone Buddhist effigies it has
spent much time and money buying at international auctions, after
they were pillaged during China's
past. It's an amazing collection.

⊙ QIANMEN 前门
☎ 6522 9384; Tiananmen Sq 天安门
广场; admission Y20; ⏰ 8.30am-4pm;
Ⓜ Qianmen
This 15th-century gate, also
known as Zhengyangmen, was
once part of the city walls that
divided the ancient inner city from
the outside world. At the time of

writing it was closed for renovations, but when open it offers a
view over Tiananmen Sq. Also
check p12.

⊙ TIANANMEN GATE (GATE OF HEAVENLY PEACE) 天安门
Tiananmen Sq 天安门广场; admission
Y15; ⏰ 8.30am-4.30pm; Ⓜ Tiananmen
Xi or Tiananmen Dong
Climb up this massive, iconic gate,
adorned with its huge Mao portrait, gaze out on Tiananmen Sq
and imagine you're China's leaders
reviewing a parade. The bag check
(Y2 to Y6 depending on size) is
compulsory. See also p12.

⊙ WORKERS' CULTURAL PALACE 劳动人民文化宫
☎ 6525 2189; Dongchang'an Jie 东长
安街; admission Y2; ⏰ 6am-10pm;
Ⓜ Tiananmen Dong
Set back from the road down an
alley, this park has an off-putting
name, but it's one of Beijing's best-
kept secrets and houses a temple
complex that was the emperor's
personal place of worship.

BEIJING MUSEUM PASS
The **Beijing Museum Pass** (博物
馆通票; www.bowuguan.bj.cn, in
Chinese; Y80) gives free or discounted
entry to most major sights. It's valid
from 1 January to 31 December of the
year you purchase it. The pass is sold
at participating museums and temples
but sells out quickly. The earlier in the
year you visit, the better your chances
of bagging one.

🛍 SHOP

🛍 BANNERMAN TANG'S TOYS & CRAFTS 盛唐轩 Toys
☎ 8404 7179; www.rbtys.com,
in Chinese; 38 Guozijian Jie
国子监街38号; ⏰ 10am-7pm;
Ⓜ Andingmen

LEGATION QUARTER WALK

The Legation Quarter was where the 19th-century foreign powers had their embassies, schools, banks and churches. The area still has a distinct European flavour, with imposing buildings set back from tree-lined streets, and it's a great place for a stroll after the hustle of nearby Tiananmen Sq. Begin at the far western end of Dongjiaomin Xiang (Map pp40–1, B8) and head east along Dongjiaomin Xiang. Look out especially for the Gothic St Michael's Church, at the junction with Taijichang Dajie, where services are still held.

Intricate, handmade toys – including miniature scenes of old Beijing – are sold here by a family who has been making toys for over 150 years. The wares work better as souvenirs than actual toys. Look for the giant toy statue outside the shop.

📖 FOREIGN LANGUAGES BOOKSTORE 外文书店 *Books*
☎ 6512 6911; 235 Wangfujing Dajie 王府井大街235号; ⏰ 9.30am-9.30pm; 🚇 Wangfujing

The shelves here groan with an ever-improving range of English-language fiction and non-fiction, as well as translations of Chinese classics and Lonely Planet guides. It's a good place to pick up a map of Beijing (Y8).

🎁 GRIFTED 贵福天地
Souvenirs
☎ 6402 0409; www.grifted.com.cn; 28 Nanluogu Xiang 南锣鼓巷28号; ⏰ 10am-10pm; 🚇 Andingmen

Slap in the middle of the trendy Nanluogu Xiang *hutong*, Grifted has a wide selection of tongue-in-cheek souvenir options, most made locally. Check out the dolls of Mao, Marx and Lenin; communist icons reinvented as soft toys. T-shirts, Mao-print cushions and quirky umbrellas are available too.

👗 LU PING TRENDSETTERS 北京贵人私ės高级成衣定制
Chinese Clothing
☎ 6402 6769; 198 Gulou Dongdajie 鼓楼东大街198号; ⏰ 9.30am-5.30pm; 🚇 Andingmen

Beautiful, hand-embroidered *qipao* (traditional Chinese dresses) can be ordered here. The quality is superb and Lu Ping is one of the few Chinese designers still specialising in making them. He does menswear too. Call ahead to make an appointment.

👕 PLASTERED T-SHIRTS 创可贴T-恤 *Clothing*
☎ 134 8884 8855; www.plasteredtshirts.com; 61 Nanluogu Xiang 南锣鼓巷61号; ⏰ 10am-10pm; 🚇 Andingmen

Rather than keeping your Beijing subway ticket, or that bottle of

Yanjing beer, as a souvenir, you can pick up a T-shirt (from Y98) that displays it, as well as shirts featuring other local icons and slogans.

☐ TEN FU'S TEA 天福茗茶 *Tea*
☎ 6524 0958; www.tenfu.com, in Chinese; 88 Wangfujing Dajie 王府井大街88号; ⏰ 10am-9pm; ⊖ Wangfujing

This Taiwanese chain has branches all over Beijing and sells countless sorts of loose tea and all manner of tea accessories. The staff will happily offer you a free tasting.

☐ ZHAOYUANGE 昭元阁 *Kites*
☎ 6512 1937; 41-3a Nanheyan Dajie 南河沿大街甲41-3号; ⏰ 10am-5pm; ⊖ Tiananmen Dong

If you want to join the masses flying kites over Tiananmen Sq or in the local parks, then come here for the array of traditional paper kites in all shapes and sizes. It sells opera masks too.

🍴 EAT

🍴 BAGUO BUYI 巴国布衣
Sichuan Y

☎ 6400 8888; 89-3 Di'anmen Dongdajie 地安门东大街 89-3号; ⏰ 11am-9.30pm; ⊖ Andingmen

Done up to resemble a traditional Chinese inn, with snippets of Peking opera performed at intervals, Baguo serves up Sichuan cuisine in a colourful and theatrical atmosphere that draws in plenty of domestic tourists. English menu.

🍴 BAIHE VEGETARIAN RESTAURANT 百合素食
Chinese Vegetarian YY

☎ 6405 2082; 23 Caoyuan Hutong, Dongzhimennei Beixiaojie 东直门内北小街草园胡同23号; ⏰ 11.30am-10pm; ⊖ Dongzhimen or Beixinqiao; ✗ Ⓥ

All Beijing's vegetarian restaurants present dishes masquerading as meat. Here, though, the

---

SCAM ALERT!
Most Beijing trips are trouble-free, but there are a few scams that visitors should be aware of. Beware of young women inviting you to a traditional tea ceremony, especially around the Qianmen area. They'll disappear before the bill comes and you'll be left with a Y2000 tab. Around Wangfujing Dajie, avoid the people who claim to be art students and want you to visit their exhibition. They're not students and the art's not worth buying. Finally, be cautious when using independent rickshaw drivers. A few have been known to drive travellers to isolated locations, before demanding more money to drive them back.

selection – lamb kebabs and Peking duck – is more imaginative than usual, and extremely tasty. Service is courteous and the atmosphere relaxed. English menu.

🍴 BEIJING DADONG ROAST DUCK RESTAURANT

北京大董烤鸭店 *Peking Duck* YY

☎ 5169 0328/29; 1st fl, Nanxincang International Plaza, 22 Dongsishitiao Lu 东四十条22号南新仓国际大厦 1层; ⏱ 11am-10pm; 🚇 Dongsishitiao

A long-term favourite with Beijingers, Dadong's hallmark bird is crispy, lean and delicious. With a large and bright dining area, this is perhaps the best place to try the capital's signature dish, but book ahead or be prepared to wait for a table. English menu.

🍴 DALI COURTYARD 大理

Yunnan YY

☎ 8404 1430; 67 Xiaojingchang Hutong, Gulou Dongdajie 鼓楼东大街小经厂胡同67号; ⏱ noon-10.30pm; 🚇 Andingmen

Idyllic on a summer evening, when you eat at tables set around the courtyard of a restored *hutong* house, this place has no menu. Instead, you pay Y100 a head and the chef decides which five or six dishes to give you.

🍴 DING DING XIANG 鼎鼎香

Chinese Hotpot Y

☎ 6417 9280; 2nd fl, Yuan Jia International Mansion, 40 Dongzhong Jie 东中街元嘉国际公寓2层; ⏱ 10.30am-10pm; 🚇 Dongsishitiao

Hotpot is a Beijing standby during the long, cold winters and one of the most sociable and fun ways to eat. You sit around a boiling pot of water, add the ingredients of your choice and cook them to your taste. Make sure to try the special, secret dipping sauce. Picture menu.

Donghuamen Night Market looking tasty (p50)

🍴 DONGHUAMEN NIGHT MARKET 东华门夜市 *Snacks* Y
Dong'anmen Dajie 东安门大街;
🕙 5.30-10.30pm; 🚇 **Wangfujing**
A favourite stop on the tourist trail and a sight in itself, the market has dozens of stallholders who will try to entice you to sample such exotic snacks as grasshoppers, scorpions and snakes. If that isn't tempting, then more conventional choices, like lamb skewers and stuffed aubergines, are available.

🍴 HUA JIA YI YUAN 花家怡园
Chinese Mixed
☎ 6405 1908; 235 Dongzhimennei Dajie **(Gui Jie)** (簋街) 东直门内大街 235号; 🕙 24hr; 🚇 **Beixinqiao**; ✗
Gui Jie, or 'ghost street', is one of Beijing's busiest restaurant strips, with all manner of hotpot and seafood eateries that stay open till the early hours. This landmark courtyard place, though, doesn't restrict itself to one type of cuisine. Instead, you can find everything from Cantonese to Peking duck here. English menu.

🍴 MAISON BOULUD 布鲁宫
French YYY
☎ 6559 9200; 23 Qianmen Dongdajie 前门东大街23号; 🕙 11.30am-10pm Mon-Fri, 11am-10pm Sat & Sun; 🚇 **Qianmen**
Located in a section of newly restored Legation Quarter build-

ings (see the boxed text, p47), the Beijing outpost of chef Daniel Boulud's empire is rated as one of the best 100 restaurants in the world. The menu and ingredients change with the seasons, the wine list is long and the service is as good as it gets in Beijing. The set lunch is a more affordable way to try the delights of this place.

🍴 SOURCE 都江园
Sichuan YY
☎ 6400 3736; 14 Banchang Hutong 板厂胡同14号; 🕙 11am-10.30pm; 🚇 **Andingmen**
A swish Sichuan restaurant, but with the spices and chillies toned down, Source is a great choice for a date, thanks to its lovely garden and pleasant service. You order from set menus that change every couple of months. English menu.

🍴 VINEYARD CAFÉ 葡萄院儿
Western Y
☎ 6402 7961; 31 Wudaoying Hutong 五道营胡同31号; 🕙 11.30am-11pm Tue-Sun; 🚇 **Yonghegong-Lama Temple**; ✗
Perfect for long, lazy weekend brunches and equally laid-back in the evening, the Vineyard has a nice conservatory, sofas to sink into, and a menu strong on salads, pizzas and Western classics like mussels in white wine. It's a few minutes' walk from the Lama Temple.

▼ DRINK
▼ DRUM & BELL
钟鼓咖啡馆 *Bar*
☎ 8403 3600; 41 Zhonglouwan Hutong
钟楼湾胡同41号; ☯ 1pm-2am;
Ⓜ Gulou Dajie

In between the Drum and Bell Towers (p39), the Drum & Bell has a splendid roof terrace that gets busy in the summer. In the winter, retreat downstairs, where there are comfy sofas. It does bar snacks as well.

▼ PASSBY BAR 过客 *Bar*
☎ 8403 8004; www.passbybar.com; 108 Nanluogu Xiang 南锣鼓巷108号; ☯ 9.30am-2am; Ⓜ Andingmen

The oldest bar on the humming *hutong* of Nanluogu Xiang, this bar-cum-restaurant is an institution and attracts locals, foreigners and travellers. Less manic than some of its competitors, it has a converted-courtyard-house setting that adds to its charm.

▼ YIN 饮 *Bar*
☎ 6523 6877; Emperor Hotel, 33 Qihelou Jie 骑河楼街33号; ☯ 11am-2am Apr-Nov; Ⓜ Dongsi

Rooftop bar with stunning views across the Forbidden City and to nearby Jingshan Park (p88). Try the house special Emperor Martini, a vodka, sake, peach and cranberry concoction. Yin is lovely at sunset, and DJs keep it lively at weekends.

★ PLAY
★ DRAGONFLY THERAPEUTIC RETREAT
悠庭保健会所 *Massage*
☎ 6527 9368; www.dragonfly.net.cn; 60 Donghuamen Dajie 东华门大街60号; ☯ 11am-1am; Ⓜ Tiananmen Dong

The two-hour Hangover Relief Massage on offer at this soothing, up-market spa works wonders, but for real pampering go for the Royal Delight, in which two masseurs get to work at the same time. Foot massages, facials and manicures are also available.

★ YUGONG YISHAN 愚公移山 *Live Music*
☎ 6404 2711; www.yugongyishan.com; West Courtyard former site of Duan Qirui Government, 3-2 Zhangzizhong Lu 张自路3-2号段祺瑞执政府旧址西院; ☯ 7pm-2am; Ⓜ Zhangzizhong Lu

Housed in a historic building that's reputed to be one of the most haunted in Beijing, the sound of the local and foreign bands, solo artists and DJs who take to the stage here will drown out the screams of the ghosts. It's perhaps the best place in the city to listen to live music.

>NORTH CHAOYANG 朝阳北

The northern part of the massive Chaoyang district is Beijing's entertainment hub and the place to head for the city's most vibrant nightlife. The bars hidden in the lanes off Sanlitun Lu, once Beijing's principal bar street, and in the nearby streets draw people from all over the city.

Southeast of Sanlitun, the area around the Workers Stadium is home to some of the capital's busiest and biggest clubs. Foodies and shopaholics are also well catered to here. With many embassies located in north Chaoyang, it has the widest selection of international restaurants in Beijing, while there's an ever-increasing number of malls and shops as well.

Sights are in short supply, but the Taoist Dongyue Temple, with its cast of demons, makes a memorable stop. Further out are the 798 Art District and the Bird's Nest Olympic Stadium, where you can pretend that you've just won a gold medal.

NORTH CHAOYANG

Please see over for map

SEE
BIRD'S NEST
鸟巢(国家体育场)
Beisihuan Zhonglu 北四环中路;
⏲ 9am-5.30pm; admission Y50;
⊙ Olympic Park

Way up in the north of Chaoyang,
the Bird's Nest Olympic Stadium,
the stunning centrepiece of the
2008 Olympics, now stands mostly
idle. It's still a remarkable, if rapidly
rusting, venue and if you want to
relive the events of August 2008,
this is the best place to do it. For
an extra Y200, you can ascend the
medals podium and make like a
winner.

C5ART 西五艺术中心
☎ 6460 3950; www.C5Art.com;
5 Sanlitun Xiwujie 三里屯西五街
5 号; ⏲ 10.30am-7pm Tue-Sun;
⊙ Agricultural Exhibition Center
This cool white space showcases
Beijing's up-and-coming artists,
especially those who are involved
in the conceptual arts. Tell the
guard at the gate you're looking
for the gallery and he'll show you
the way.

DONGYUE TEMPLE
东岳庙
☎ 6551 0151; 141 Chaoyangmenwai
Dajie 朝阳门外大街141号;
admission Y10; ⏲ 8.30am-4.30pm Tue-
Sun; ⊙ Chaoyangmen

Beijing's most morbid temple,
Dongyue is populated by hundreds of life-sized ghoul and ghost
statues, who offer protection from
harassment in the netherworld in
return for devotion and a suitable
offering. Still a working Taoist
temple, Dongyue is dedicated to
the God of Taishan (one of China's
five holy mountains).

SHOP
ROUGE BAISER
Clothing, Homewares
☎ 6464 3530; www.rougebaiser-elise
.com; 5 Sanlitun Xiwujie 三里屯西五
街5号; ⏲ 11am-7pm Mon, 10am-7pm
Tue-Sun; ⊙ Agricultural Exhibition
Center
Sumptuous sheets, cute kiddies'
clothes, and posh pyjamas and
kimonos are sold here, all created
by a Shanghai-based French
designer.

SANLITUN YASHOW
CLOTHING MARKET
三里屯雅秀市场 *Clothing,
Market*
☎ 6416 8945; 58 Gongrentiyuchang
Beilu 工人体育场北路58号;
⏲ 10am-9pm; ⊙ Tuanjiehu
Along with south Chaoyang's Silk
Market (p76), this five-storey
emporium is a travellers' favourite
for clothes, outdoor gear, shoes,
silk and bags. Haggle hard here.

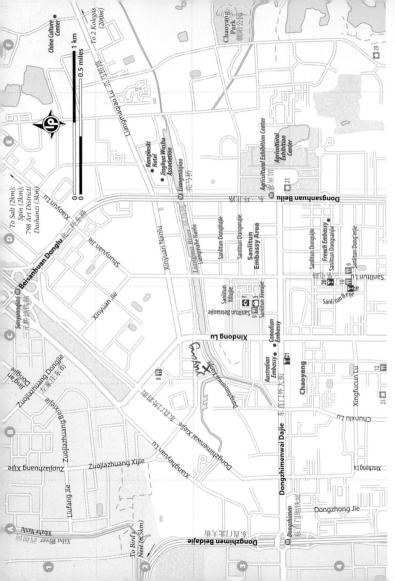

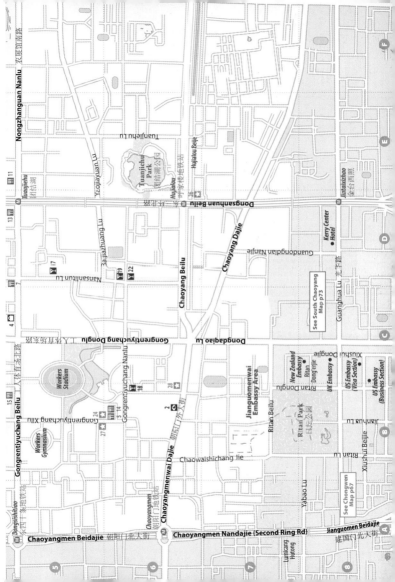

WORTH THE TRIP – THE 798 ART DISTRICT

The 798 Art District (大山子艺术区), also known as Dashanzi, sits in northeastern Chaoyang; see p16. Some of the most important galleries here include **Galleria Continua** (☎ 5978 9505; www.galleriacontinua.com; 2 Jiuxianqiao Lu 酒仙桥路2号大山子艺术区; ☒ 11am-6pm Tue-Sun), which specialises in Chinese installation and video art, and **Amelie Gallery** (☎ 5978 9698; www.longyibang.com; 2 Jiuxianqiao Lu 酒仙桥路2号大山子艺术区; ☒ 10am-7pm Tue-Sun), a great place to check out contemporary Chinese painters. Head to the **MR Gallery** (☎ 5978 9058; www.mrgallery.com.cn; 2 Jiuxianqiao Lu 酒仙桥路2号大山子艺术区; ☒ 11am-6pm Tue-Sun) for photography from China and abroad.

Dashanzi also houses some excellent shops. **Timezone 8** (☎ 5978 9072; www.timezone8.com; 4 Jiuxianqiao Lu 酒仙桥路4号大山子艺术区; ☒ 11am-7.30pm) has Beijing's best selection of books (in all languages) on Chinese contemporary art and artists, as well as titles and magazines on world art, architecture, cinema and design.

There are several cafes, bars and restaurants among the galleries; many have eye-catching decor, like the artfully designed **At Café** (☎ 5978 9942; 4 Jiuxianqiao Lu 酒仙桥路4号大山子艺术区; ☒ 11am-midnight), which has gaping holes in its interior walls, as well as a menu of Western favourites like pasta and tempting desserts. The nearby **No 6 Sichuan Food Studio** (☎ 5978 9623; 4 Jiuxianqiao Lu 酒仙桥路4号大山子艺术区; ☒ 11am-9pm) is a shrine to fiery Sichuan cuisine beneath a lurid pink statue of Mao Zedong.

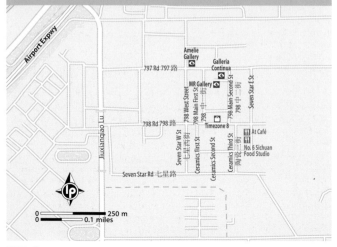

☐ SPIN 旋 *Ceramics*
☎ 6437 8649; 6 Fangyuan Xilu 芳园西路6号; ⏱ 11am-9.30pm;
⊙ Sanyuanqiao

Fantastic, quirky ceramics are the order of the day here. There are gorgeous, odd-shaped vases, long plates and all manner of striking household items. It's just off Fangyuan Xilu; look for the long, single-storey brick building.

🍴 EAT

🍴 BELLAGIO 鹿港小镇
Taiwanese   Y
☎ 6551 3533; 6 Gongrentiyuchang Xilu 工人体育场西路6号; ⏱ 11am-5am;
⊙ Chaoyangmen

Don't be fooled by the Italian name; Bellagio is a slick Taiwanese chain that has great coffee, *baobing* (shaved-ice) desserts and an extensive menu of Taiwanese classics, such as three-cup chicken. After midnight, it's busy with the clubbers from the nearby dance dens.

🍴 BOCATA *Cafe*   Y
☎ 6417 5291; 3 Sanlitun Lu 三里屯北路3号; ⏱ 11am-midnight;
⊙ Tuanjiehu

Great spot for coffee or lunch, especially in the summer when the outdoor terrace gets crowded. There's a vaguely Middle Eastern

theme to the food: falafels and decent hummus, but the sandwiches on ciabatta and top-class chips are decidedly Western in flavour.

🍴 ELEMENT FRESH
北京新元素餐厅 *Western*   YY
☎ 6417 1318; 3rd fl, Bldg 8, Village, 19 Sanlitun Lu 三里屯路19号Village 南区8号楼8-3-3单元; ⏱ 11am-11pm Mon-Fri, 8am-11pm Sat & Sun;
⊙ Tuanjiehu; ✂

Packed at weekends, Element Fresh has a mix of healthy and hefty salads, sandwiches and MSG-free mains that's made It one of the most popular spots in Sanlitun. There's a large outside terrace and wi-fi too.

🍴 HAITANGHUA PYONGYANG COLD NOODLE RESTAURANT
平壤海棠花冷面馆 *Korean*   Y
☎ 6461 6295/6298; 8 Xinyuanxili Zhongjie 新源西里中街8号;
⏱ 11.30am-10.30pm;
⊙ Liangmaqiao

There aren't too many North Korean restaurants in the world and a night here is made special by the waitresses who take it in turns to break out into Korean folk and pop songs. The picture menu is heavy on Korean hotpot and, of course, noodles. The restaurant is on the corner of Xindong Lu.

Lu Zhengyuan
Sculptor and painter whose work has been exhibited across Asia, Australia, Europe and the USA

Why is Beijing such a happening place for artists now? Beijing's not like the rest of China and at the same time it's not like a foreign city. There are lots of conflicts here and that means there are lots of possibilities to create.
Do ordinary Beijingers respect artists? Ten years ago, when the art market wasn't so hot, they looked down on artists. Now, they think we're all rich.
What about the government's attitude to artists? On the one hand, the government would like to exploit the success of contemporary artists. On the other hand, they're also a bit scared of art's potential to cause trouble, so they want to control it. **What Beijing art museums would you recommend to a visitor?** I don't think the museums have anything to do with contemporary art; they all reflect the CCP's policies. But there are a lot of independent galleries and they act like museums. Visiting them is the best way to see Chinese contemporary art.

DISTRICTS

NORTH CHAOYANG

🍴 HERBAL CAFÉ
泰和草本工坊 *Cantonese*   Y
☎ 6416 0618; 3rd fl, Village, 19
Sanlitun Lu 三里屯路19号Village 3层;
🕐 11am-11pm; 🚇 Tuanjiehu
Comfortable, MSG-free restaurant, where you can eat in a mock-up of one of Hong Kong's famous trams. It's a good spot for cheap dim sum, soups (which come in cool canisters), and Cantonese desserts like Portuguese egg tarts. There's a decent range of teas too.

🍴 JENNY LOU'S 捷妮璐 *Deli*   Y
☎ 6461 6928, 6 Sanlitun Beixiaojie
三里屯北小街6号; 🕐 8am-10pm;
🚇 Agricultural Exhibition Center
In the heart of the embassy district, this popular deli has an impressive range of cold cuts, cheeses and wine, as well as all sorts of other Western staples.

🍴 MOSTO 摸石头 *European*   YY
☎ 5208 6030; 3rd fl, Nali Patio, 81
Sanlitun Lu 三里屯北路81号那里花园3层; 🕐 noon-10.30pm;
🚇 Tuanjiehu; 🍴
Patronised by the staff from nearby embassies and the ladies-who-lunch crowd, Mosto serves up solid, well-presented dishes with a vaguely Mediterranean theme. There's a good wine list, excellent desserts and attractive set-lunch deals.

🍴 PURE LOTUS VEGETARIAN
净心莲 *Chinese Vegetarian*   YY
☎ 6592 3627; inside Zhongguo
Wenlianyuan, 12 Nongzhanguan Nanlu
农展馆南路12号长虹桥农业部西
侧通广大厦院内; 🕐 11am-11pm;
🚇 Tuanjiehu; 🍴 🅥
A very smart, monk-run establishment, where the chefs do wonders with a mix of soybeans, tofu and vegetables. The dishes have wonderful names like 'The ordinary one with virtue holds lightning'. It's located in a forecourt just off Nongzhanguan Nanlu.

🍴 PURPLE HAZE 紫苏庭 *Thai* Y
☎ 6413 0899; opposite north gate of
the Workers Stadium 工人体育场
北门对面胡同; 🕐 10am-midnight;
🚇 Dongsishitiao; 🍴
Beijing's trendiest Thai, with a reliable take on Thai classics like tom yum soup and red and green curries. The tangy, spicy salads are especially good. But the purple decor takes a bit of getting used to. It's down an alley; look for the branch of the ICBC bank.

🍴 RUMI 入迷 *Persian*   Y
☎ 8454 3838; www.rumigrill.com;
1a Gongrentiyuchang Beilu 工体北
路甲1号; 🕐 11.30am-midnight;
🚇 Tuanjiehu
Located in a strip of Middle Eastern restaurants, Rumi's white,

minimalist interior is belied by its warm service, great shish kebabs and authentic Iranian stews. It doesn't serve alcohol, but you can bring your own.

🍴 SALT 盐 *Fusion* ¥¥
☎ 6437 8457; 1st fl, 9 Jiangtai Xilu 将台西路北铂丽酒店对面; ⏰ noon-10.30pm; 🚇 Sanyuanqiao; ✗
This stylish but relaxed restaurant is dominated by its open kitchen and is perhaps the best place in town for contemporary Western cuisine. The food is a mix of Mediterranean and South American styles. It's just west of the Rosedale Hotel. Book ahead.

🍴 THREE GUIZHOU MEN 三个贵州人 *Guizhou* ¥
☎ 6551 8517; Gongrentiyuchang Xilu 工人体育场西路; ⏰ 24hr; 🚇 Chaoyangmen

CHINESE RESTAURANT ETIQUETTE
> Don't stick your chopsticks vertically into your rice bowl; it's believed to resemble an omen of death.
> Never serve yourself tea or drinks without filling the cups of your fellow diners first.
> Don't let the spout of a teapot face anyone; it's considered rude.
> Never point your chopsticks at people or wave them around. It's regarded as bad manners.

The spicy but sour cuisine of Guizhou province in southwest China is delicious. Try the sour-fish hotpot, or the sublime pork ribs and the tremendous smashed potato. To get here, walk down the lane to the side of Bellagio (p57), turn left at the end, enter the building with the elevator and go to the 2nd floor, where you'll be greeted by a hostess with a silver headdress.

🍴 XINJIANG RED ROSE RESTAURANT 新疆红玫瑰餐厅 *Xinjiang* ¥
☎ 6415 5741; 5 Xingfuyicun 工人体育场北门对面,幸福一村5号; ⏰ 11am-11pm; 🚇 Dongsishitiao
Eating here is like hanging out at a raucous party. Communal seating is at long canteen-style tables, and when the Uighur music and dancers get going (from 7.30pm to 9pm) it's very loud. The menu is mutton dominated. It's down an alley opposite the north gate of the Workers' Stadium, next to Bodhi (p63).

🍸 DRINK
🍸 BAR BLU 蓝吧 *Bar*
☎ 6417 4124; 4th fl, Tongli Studios, Sanlitun Beijie 三里屯北街同里4层; ⏰ 4pm-late; 🚇 Tuanjiehu
Perennially popular with a younger crowd who flock to the oversubscribed rooftop terrace in the summer, Bar Blu also has a

small dance floor, a Wednesday-night quiz and karaoke on Sunday. The daily happy hour runs from 4pm to 9pm.

BOOKWORM 书虫 *Cafe*

☎ 6586 9507; www.beijingbookworm .com; Bldg 4, Nansanlitun Lu 南三里屯路4号楼; 🕐 9am-2am; 🔘 Tuanjiehu;
A hub of Beijing expat life, the Bookworm is both an English-language lending library and an up-market cafe. It's the place to hear visiting authors talk, hunker

down over the laptop, browse the huge library or kick back over coffee, cocktails and food. Head to the roof terrace in the summer.

FACE 妃思 *Bar*

☎ 6551 6788; 26 Dongcaoyuan, Gongrentiyuchang Nanlu 工体南路东草园26号; 🕐 6pm-late; 🔘 Chaoyangmen
A stylish series of intercon-nected rooms with a Southeast Asian theme, Face is refreshingly unpretentious. It's a place to sip cocktails or pints of Guinness.

The school library was never like this; the Bookworm cafe even hosts visiting authors

Echo Sun
Co-owner of Q Bar (opposite) and Beijing's best-known bartender

How did you start making cocktails? When I was a student working in a bar. Back then, people mostly drank long drinks, like gin and tonic, and I found making them boring, so I bought a book and started learning how to mix proper cocktails. **What's the hardest cocktail to make?** I think a martini. It doesn't have many ingredients, but getting the right balance is hard. **How has Beijing's bar scene changed since you opened Q Bar in 2006?** People care a lot more about the quality of drinks, which wasn't the case three or four years ago. But the biggest change is that a lot more locals are going to bars. When we opened in 2006, our customers were 80% foreigners. Now, it's half locals and half foreigners. **Where do you go out?** I like some of the Japanese bars that have opened recently. But they can't make a dirty martini like I can.

There's an outdoor terrace and two pool tables.

�Y GLEN *Bar*
☎ 6591 1191; 203 Taiyue Haoting, 16 Nansanlitun Lu 南三里屯路16号 泰悦豪庭2层203; ☯ 6pm-2am; ⓜ Tuanjiehu

Beijing's finest and most extensive selection of whiskies combine with painstaking attention to detail – think shaved ice cubes – to make this Japanese-style bar a spot for drinking connoisseurs. It's on the 2nd floor; take the stairs on the right of the building.

�Y MESH *Bar*
☎ 6417 6688; 1st fl, opposite House Hotel, Village, 11 Sanlitun Lu 三里 屯路11号瑜舍一层; ☯ 5pm-1am; ⓜ Tuanjiehu

Designed to within an inch of its life, Mesh is achingly trendy with fancy light fittings, a white bar and mesh screens separating the different areas. But it's still fun and the bartenders know their stuff. On Thursday, it's gay friendly.

�Y PADDY O'SHEA'S
爱尔兰酒吧 *Bar*
☎ 6415 6389; 28 Dongzhimenwai Dajie 东直门外大街28号; ☯ 10am-2am; ⓜ Dongzhimen

It gets packed when there's a big game on – this is a key place for watching sport – so get here early

and grab a spot at the bar, or head upstairs, where there's a pool table. It does pub grub, and the daily happy hour runs till 8pm.

�Y Q BAR Q吧 *Bar*
☎ 6595 9239; www.qbarbeijing.com; 6th fl, Eastern Inn Hotel, Nansanlitun Lu 南三 里屯路; ☯ 6pm-late; ⓜ Tuanjiehu

Unselfconsciously cool, Q Bar is one of Beijing's hot spots and is hopping at weekends. Thankfully, there's room to spread out inside, or you can head to the excellent rooftop terrace. There's a big 'Q' hanging off the side of the Eastern Inn Hotel to guide you there.

�Y SADDLE CANTINA *Bar*
☎ 5208 6005; West Wing, Nali Patio, 81 Sanlitun Lu 三里屯北路81号那里花 园2层; ☯ 10am-2am; ⓜ Tuanjiehu

Sanlitun is hardly down Mexico way, but after a few of its potent margaritas you might think it is. Burritos and fajitas are made too, and the place is always heaving with a 20-something crowd.

★ PLAY

★ BODHI 菩提会所 *Massage*
☎ 6417 9595; www.bodhi.com.cn; 17 Gongrentiyuchang Beilu 工人体育 场北路17号(体育场北门对面); ☯ 11am-12.30am; ⓜ Dongsishitiao

This serene, up-scale spa is the perfect place to rejuvenate after

DISTRICTS

NORTH CHAOYANG

a hard day pounding Beijing's streets. There are great Chinese or Thai massages, as well as wraps and facials. The foot reflexology massages are especially good. There are 40% discounts before 5pm during the week. It's opposite the north gate of the Workers Stadium.

☆ CARGO *Club*
☎ 6551 6898/78; 6 Gongrentiyuchang Xilu 工人体育场西路6号; cover charge Y50; ⏱ 8pm-late; Ⓜ Chaoyangmen
Young and fashionable Beijingers flock to this place, located in the cluster of clubs just south of the west gate of the Workers Stadium.

KARAOKE
Karaoke bars (known as 'KTV') are everywhere in Beijing. They're where Beijingers go to unwind after work and to celebrate. Renting a room to wail out the latest mando-pop hits with your friends might seem odd to Westerners at first, but once you get over the shyness of singing in public (alcohol helps), karaoke is a lot of fun and surprisingly cathartic. The best way to try it is with some locals; otherwise head to **Melody** (☎ 6551 0808; A-77 Chaoyangmenwai Dajie; rooms per hr from Y79; ⏱ 8am-2am), which has a selection of English-language tunes as well as snacks and drinks. If you're lucky, the staff might help you out with some backing vocals.

Big-name DJs from abroad play here on a regular basis and it's busier during the week than its rivals.

☆ CD JAZZ CAFÉ 北京 CD爵士俱乐部 *Live Music*
☎ 6506 8288; 16 Dongsanhuan Beilu 东三环北16路; ⏱ 4pm-2am; Ⓜ Agricultural Exhibition Center
There are live performances every Thursday, Friday and Saturday, as well as swing dancing on Monday. It's by the overpass south of the Agricultural Exhibition Center.

☆ CHAOYANG THEATRE 朝阳剧场 *Acrobatics, Peking Opera*
☎ 6507 2421; 36 Dongsanhuan Beilu 东三环北路36号; tickets Y180-680; performances 5.15pm & 7.30pm; Ⓜ Hujialou
The most accessible venue to catch an acrobatics show, with splendid daily performances by visiting troupes from all over China.

☆ DESTINATION 目的地 *Club*
☎ 6551 5138; www.bjdestination.com; 7 Gongrentiyuchang Xilu 工人体育场西路7号; cover charge Fri & Sat Y60; ⏱ 8pm-late; Ⓜ Chaoyangmen
This grey concrete block might not look enticing, and the interior decor isn't much better, but as Beijing's only genuine gay club it's jammed every weekend with boys

who like boys and girls who want a break from them.

⭐ 2 KOLEGAS 两个好朋友
Live Music

☎ 6436 8998; www.2kolegas.com; 21 Liangmaqiao Lu 亮马桥路21号(汽车电影院内); ⏰ 8pm-2am Mon-Sat, 10am-9pm Sun; Ⓜ Liangmaqiao

Underground rock and punk acts rule at this ramshackle but endearing club. It's inside a drive-in movie theatre – to get here head about 1500m down the driveway from Liangmaqiao Lu. The venue is hidden behind the big, colourful restaurant to the left of the drive-in.

⭐ WORLD OF SUZIE WONG
苏西黄 *Club*

☎ 6500 3377; www.suziewong.com.cn; 1a Nongzhanguan Nanlu 农展馆路甲1号; ⏰ 7pm-late; Ⓜ Tuanjiehu

Still jumping most nights of the week, Suzie Wong's opium-den chic with a 21st-century twist has made it a Beijing nightlife legend. The dance floor, roof terrace and traditional Chinese-style beds you can lounge on attract a really mixed crowd, from models to business types and working girls. The entrance is just by the west gate of Chaoyang Park.

>CHONGWEN 崇文

Historically, Chongwen was a poor part of Beijing that housed the sorts of establishments, like brothels and theatres, which were banned from the imperial city. Even now, Chongwen remains a low-key district that lacks the new skyscrapers and malls that have transformed its more glamorous neighbours.

But if you believe that's a reason not to visit, then think again. Chongwen might be short on attractions, but what it does have is unmissable. The Temple of Heaven Park, one of Beijing's most essential sights, occupies a huge chunk of the district's west side. Nearby, the Pearl Market is a five-storey shrine to semi-precious stones and jewellery, and Chongwen is home to some of Beijing's best Peking duck restaurants.

There are also still pockets of traditional life in Chongwen. Check out the area bordered by Qianmen Dajie, Qinian Dajie, Zhushikou Dongdajie and Qianmen Dongdajie, where a vibrant, if ramshackle, *hutong* (alleyway) community continues to defy the wrecking ball.

CHONGWEN

👁 SEE
Beijing Planning
  Exhibition Hall 1 A2
Longtan Park 2 D4
Ming City Wall
  Ruins Park 3 C2
Red Gate Gallery ....(see 4)
Southeast
  Watchtower 4 D2

Temple of Heaven
  Park 5 A4

🛍 SHOP
Pearl Market 6 B4

🍴 EAT
Bianyifang Roast Duck
  Restaurant 7 B3

Duyichu 8 A3
Liqun Roast Duck
  Restaurant 9 A2

⭐ PLAY
Red Theatre 10 C4

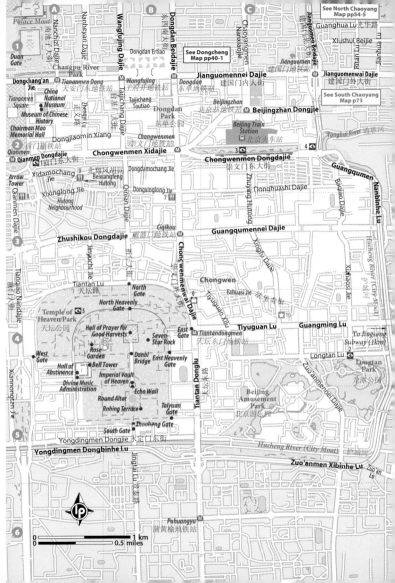

DISTRICTS

CHONGWEN

👁 SEE

👁 BEIJING PLANNING EXHIBITION HALL
北京市规划展览馆

☎ 6701 7074; 20 Qianmen Dongdajie
前门东大街20号; admission Y30;
🕐 9am-5pm Tue-Sun; 🚇 Qianmen

If you want an overview of Beijing's extraordinary transformation from walled city to modern metropolis, this is the place to come. Compare the 1949 bronze map of the city with the huge diorama of the current Beijing. It's a good way to put the scale of the place into perspective.

👁 LONGTAN PARK 龙潭公园

☎ 6716 7319; Longtan Lu 龙潭路; admission Y2; 🕐 6am-10pm, last entry 9.30pm; 🚇 Tiantandongmen or Jingsong

One of Beijing's nicest parks, artfully landscaped Longtan has bridges, pavilions, playgrounds for kids and a waterfall. Escape the summer heat by hiring a boat (Y60 per hour, Y200 deposit) and cruising the large artificial lake that dominates it.

👁 MING CITY WALL RUINS PARK 明城墙遗址公园

Chongwenmen Dongdajie 崇文门东大街; admission free; 🕐 24hr; 🚇 Chongwenmen

UNDERGROUND BEIJING

Spooked by the prospect of nuclear war with the Russians, in 1969 Mao ordered the construction of a massive labyrinth of tunnels and bomb shelters under the heart of the city. It took 10 years for them to be built, by which time Mao was dead and the threat of nuclear annihilation had receded. Until recently, it was still possible to visit some of the tunnels running under Chongwen. Safety fears saw them closed permanently in early 2008. But it is rumoured that parts of the network, which stretched as far as the Summer Palace (p14) are still used by the government for clandestine purposes.

As late as the early 1950s, Beijing was still a walled city. Now, all that remains of the fortifications is this slender strip of restored wall in a small park. Follow the footpath along it, and check out the bullet holes in some of the bricks.

👁 RED GATE GALLERY
红门画廊

☎ 6525 1005; www.redgategallery.com; Dongbianmen 东便门; 🕐 10am-5pm; 🚇 Jianguomen or Chongwenmen

When it opened in 1991, Red Gate was Beijing's first gallery devoted to Chinese contemporary art. With its stunning watchtower setting (opposite), Red Gate remains one of the most influential art spaces in the city. It's located on the tower's 1st floor; you usually don't need to pay the tower's admission fee to visit.

☉ SOUTHEAST WATCHTOWER
东南角楼

☎ 8512 1554; Dongbianmen 东便门; **admission Y10;** ⏱ 8am-5.30pm; ⓜ **Jianguomen or Chongwenmen**

This Ming-era watchtower has 144 archer windows but is also notable for the 'I was here' graffiti left by international troops during the 1900 Boxer Rebellion. On the tower's 2nd floor there are historical exhibits about Chongwen district. With the admission ticket, you're allowed to walk the 100m stretch of old city wall attached to the tower.

☉ TEMPLE OF HEAVEN PARK
天坛公园

☎ 6701 2483; North Gate, Tiantan Donglu 天坛东路北门; **park & temple complex Y30, park only Y10;** ⏱ **sights 8am-6pm, last entry 5pm, park 6am-9pm, last entry 8pm;** ⓜ **Tiantandongmen**

From 1420 until the fall of imperial China, successive emperors travelled here to pray for good harvests. Nowadays, it swarms with both tourists and locals. At dawn, the park turns into a vast stage for taichi; later on the

DISTRICTS

CHONGWEN

Temple of Heaven, one of Beijing's favourite historical sights, sits in the Temple of Heaven Park

visitors arrive to gaze in awe at one of Beijing's most iconic sights (see p18). Audio-guides are Y40.

🛍 SHOP

🛍 PEARL MARKET 红桥市场
Market

☎ 6713 3354; 36 Tiantan Lu 天坛路 36号; ⏰ 9am-7pm;
🚇 Tiantandongmen

Home to more pearls than the South Seas, this crowded emporium houses its cheaper specimens on the 3rd floor. Better quality, and more pricy, pearls can be found on the 4th and 5th floors. The market's roof garden

offers a view of the Temple of Heaven (p69).

🍴 EAT

🍴 BIANYIFANG ROAST DUCK RESTAURANT 便宜坊烤鸭店
Peking Duck   YY

☎ 6712 0505; 3rd fl, China New World Shopping Mall, 5 Chongwenmenwai Dajie 崇文门外大街5号新世界商场二期 三层; 🚇 Chongwenmen; ✂

Dating back to the Qing era, Bianyifang claims to be the original Peking duck restaurant. It cooks its birds in a closed oven, as opposed to a half-open one, and the meat is juicy and tender. The menu also

So many pearls at the Pearl Market, but head upstairs if you're looking for the best quality ones

QIANMEN DAJIE

Given a massive overhaul for the 2008 Olympics, the newly pedestrianised Qianmen Dajie is meant to resemble a late-Qing-dynasty shopping street that will attract tourists by the busload. It hasn't worked out that way. At the time of writing, many shops were still unoccupied, leaving bemused visitors with little to do except ride the reproduction trams up and down the street, or take pictures of the rebuilt Qianmen Decorative Arch.

offers duck-liver and heart dishes; just about any part of the bird that is edible is available here.

🍴 DUYICHU 都一处

Chinese Dumplings Y

☎ 6702 1671; 38 Qianmen Dajie 前门大街38号; ⏱ 7.30am-9pm; 🚇 Qianmen

Another Qing-dynasty hangover, this place specialises in *shaomai*, the delicate dumplings that originated in eastern China. They're delightful little bundles of meat, fish or vegetables, so be prepared to queue for a table at weekends.

🍴 LIQUN ROAST DUCK RESTAURANT 利群烤鸭店

Peking Duck YY

☎ 6702 5681, 6705 5578; 11 Beixiangfeng Hutong 前门东大街正义路南口北翔凤胡同11号; ⏱ 10am-10pm; 🚇 Qianmen

The duck here is so prized that you have to call a day ahead to reserve both a bird and a table (otherwise, turn up at off-peak times and be prepared to wait an hour). Buried down a crumbling *hutong,* the restaurant itself has seen better days, but the duck is delicious and comes with all the trimmings.

⭐ PLAY

☆ RED THEATRE 红剧场

Kung Fu

☎ 6710 3671; 44 Xingfu Dajie 幸福大街44号; tickets Y180-680; ⏱ 5.15pm & 7.30pm; 🚇 Tiantandongmen

This theatre's long-running *The Legend of Kung Fu* production depicts a boy's journey to kung fu master. It's like a flashy Broadway musical except the story is propelled by thrilling kung fu moves instead of song-and-dance numbers.

>SOUTH CHAOYANG 朝阳南

Chaoyang south of Ritan Park has undergone the mother of all make-overs in recent years. Posh apartment and office complexes have sprung up in the central business district (CBD), and in their wake have come fashionable eateries and bars. The extraordinary and spectacular CCTV building dominates the CBD, which is located just northeast of Jian-guomenwai Dajie, and makes a great landmark for visitors.

But south Chaoyang is also one of Beijing's premier shopping zones. The Panjiayuan Antique Market heaves at weekends with locals and visitors searching for hidden treasures, while the Silk Market's huge range of knock-off goods draws crowds every day. There are also up-scale malls, housing the best local fashion designers and foreign labels.

New subway line 10 cuts north–south through the area, while the venerable line 1 runs east–west. They're a better option than taxis during the day, when the roads here are super-busy.

SOUTH CHAOYANG

👁 SEE

👁 CCTV BUILDING 央视大楼
Dongsanhuan Zhonglu 东三环中路;
🚇 **Guomao**

The new headquarters for China Central TV is like no other building in the city, or anywhere else. This Dutch-designed behemoth, with its open centre, seemingly defies gravity. The cheeky locals call it 'big shorts', as it reminds them of a pair of trousers. See also p20.

👁 RITAN PARK 日坛公园
☎ **6592 5576; Ritan Lu** 日坛路;
admission free; 🕑 **6am-9pm;**
🚇 **Chaoyangmen or Yonganli**

One of Beijing's oldest and most pleasant parks, pine-tree-lined Ritan was where emperors made sacrifices to the sun. These days, it's taichi practitioners and kids playing who mainly use the large ritual altar at the north end of the park.

COMMUNIST KITSCH
Mao memorabilia remains one of Beijing's most popular souvenirs and is sold everywhere there are tourists. Vendors say Mao's *Little Red Book,* a collection of his quotations, is still the number-one seller. But if that doesn't do it for you, you can find Mao watches and 1970s-era alarm clocks, or lighters emblazoned with the Great Helmsman's image that play the Chinese national anthem, at Panjiayuan Antique Market (p76).

👁 ZHIHUA TEMPLE 智化寺
☎ **6525 0072; 5 Lumicang Hutong** 禄米仓胡同5号; **admission Y20;**
🕑 **9am-4.30pm Tue-Sun;**
🚇 **Jianguomen or Chaoyangmen**

With its distinctive black-tiled roofs and an air of dilapidated grandeur, this little-visited Ming-era temple is an oasis of calm in the busy downtown area. The highlight is the Tathagata Hall, with its cabinets for storing sutras and statues of the Sakyamuni Buddha.

🛍 SHOP

🏠 BEIJING CURIO CITY 北京古玩城 *Market*
☎ **6774 7711; 21 Dongsanhuan Nanlu** 东三环南路21号; 🕑 **10am-6pm;**
🚇 **Jingsong**

Four floors of antiques, jewellery, ceramics, carpets and furniture are available here, in a more low-key atmosphere than in many Beijing markets. Not all the antiques are the real deal, though, so look carefully before you buy and haggle as hard as you can.

🏠 FIVE COLOURS EARTH 五色土 *Clothing*
☎ **5869 2923; 2505, 25th fl, Bldg 14, Jianwai Soho, 39 Dongsanhuan Zhonglu** 东三环中路39号建外 SOHO 14号楼25层2505 ;
🕑 **9am-6pm;** 🚇 **Guomao**

He Hongyu
Fashion designer and owner of Five Colours Earth (opposite)

How would you describe the clothes you design? They're not really traditional, although we use traditional embroidery. I think I take elements of classic Chinese clothing and mix them with Western styles. **Why do you use embroidery from Guizhou province in all your designs?** I think that embroidery is a really valuable treasure of our country. I wanted to help preserve it and I think creating a market for it is the best way to do that. **Can you compare the way women dress in Beijing now with when you were growing up here in the 1970s?** Well, when I was young there was no such thing as fashion in Beijing. Now, women have so many more choices and they dress much more sexily. **Are Beijing women the most fashionable in China?** I think so. In Shanghai, the women mostly want to wear Western labels and they wear what the magazines tell them to. Beijing women are more open-minded and independent.

DISTRICTS

SOUTH CHAOYANG

Hip tops, skirts and jackets with a traditional Chinese twist. The designer is a Beijinger who incorporates elaborate embroidery unique to the Miao minority in southwest China into her clothes. Most of the stock is sold overseas; you can pick it up far cheaper here.

🛍 MUSHI 模西 Clothing
☎ 6568 0036; www.mushi.com.cn; 1st fl, LG Twin Towers Shopping Mall B-12, Jianguomenwai Dajie 建国门外大街乙12号LG双子座大厦1层; ⏰ 10am-8pm Mon-Sat; 🚇 Yonganli
French-born Caroline Deleens lived in China as a teenager and has returned to Beijing with her own clothing line that mixes cool, sexy European styles with traditional Chinese fabrics, especially silk.

🛍 PANJIAYUAN ANTIQUE MARKET 潘家园古玩市场
Antiques & Collectables
☎ 6775 2405; Panjiayuan Lu 潘家园路; ⏰ 8.30am-6pm Mon-Fri, 4.30am-6pm Sat & Sun; 🚇 Jingsong
Beijing's most beloved flea market sells almost every Chinese knick-knack imaginable. It's a great spot for souvenirs, but bargain hard and treat any claims of antiquity with scepticism. Not much goes on here during the week. Instead, get here early on the weekends for one of the most fun shopping experiences in Beijing. Also see p22.

🛍 SHARD BOX STORE 慎德阁
Jewellery
☎ 8561 3712; 1 Ritan Beilu 日坛北路1号; ⏰ 9am-7pm; 🚇 Yonganli
Exquisite shard boxes in all sizes are on offer at this family-run store. They're beautiful and unique pieces, made with porcelain fragments from Ming- and Qing-dynasty vases destroyed during the Cultural Revolution. Prices start low but go high. It also sells jewellery, mostly sourced from Tibet and Mongolia.

🛍 SILK MARKET 秀水市场
Market
☎ 6501 8811; Jianguomenwai Dajie 建国门外大街; ⏰ 9am-9pm; 🚇 Yonganli

THE SILK MARKET HARD SELL
With coachloads of tourists arriving at the Silk Market (above) every day, you have to be a very canny shopper to get the better of the vendors here. The stalls are staffed by English-speaking young women from south-eastern Anhui province, who will alternately flatter and browbeat you into both buying their goods and accepting a price that is over the odds. Men will be told how handsome they are, women how that top is exactly the right size. And because they do it at speed, you'll have handed over the cash before you even know it.

The six-storey Silk Market is one of the most popular in Beijing, thanks to its wide array of high-quality fakes of big-name brands. Always packed, it's best for clothes, but you can find bags and electronics here too. The silk is on the 3rd floor and is one of the few genuine items sold here.

🍴 EAT

🍴 DIN TAI FUNG 鼎泰丰
Chinese Dumplings   *YY*
☎ 6553 1536; 6th fl, Shin Kong Pl, 87 Jianguo Lu 建国路87号新光天地6层; ⏰ 11.30am-9.30pm Mon-Fri, 11am-10pm Sat & Sun; ⓜ Dawanglu; ✖
Very special dumplings are the draw here; the original restaurant of this Taiwanese chain was once hailed as one of the 10 best in the world. Try the *xiaolongbao*; thin-skinned packages with meat or vegie fillings that are surrounded by a superb, scalding soup. It has English menu.

🍴 GRANDMA'S KITCHEN
祖母的厨房 *American*   *Y*
☎ 6503 2893; 11 Xiushui Nanjie 秀水南街11号; ⏰ 7.30am-11pm; ⓜ Yonganli; ✖ Ⓥ
Popular with families and those pining for authentic American comfort food like meat loaf, burgers and pancakes, this home-style

A shimmer of silken bolts at the Silk Market

restaurant's big breakfasts will set you up for the day. English menu; friendly staff.

🍴 HATSUNE 隐泉日本料理
Japanese   *YY*
☎ 6581 3939; 2nd fl, Heqiao Bldg C, 8a Guanghua Lu 光华路甲8号和乔大厦C座2层; ⏰ 11am-2pm & 5.30-10pm; ⓜ Jintaixizhao or Dawanglu; ✖
Offering delicious food in a stylish setting, Hatsune is more like a Californian sushi joint than a traditional Japanese place. The house-speciality hand rolls have names like Ninja and the aptly-titled King Kong. There's a generous set lunch deal here.

MAKYE AME 玛吉阿米
Tibetan   Y
☎ 6506 9616; www.makyeame.cn;
2nd fl, 11a Xiushui Nanjie 秀水南街
甲11号2层; ⏱ 11.30am-midnight;
🚇 Yonganli
With its daily floor show of Tibetan
dancing, this is a loud and fun
place that serves up lots of yak
meat, *momo* (Tibetan dumplings)
and *tsampa,* the roasted barley
meal that is a Tibetan staple, in
a welcoming atmosphere. Book
ahead at weekends.

MARE 古老海西餐厅
Spanish   YY
☎ 6595 4178/2890; 1st fl, e-Tower, 12c
Guanghua Lu 光华路12C数码01大
厦一层南侧; ⏱ 11.30am-11.30pm;
🚇 Guomao; ✗
The location – the ground floor
of an office building – might be
odd, but that doesn't stop the
CBD crowd flocking here for
the 30 types of authentic tapas,
including sizzling garlic prawns
and salty cod, and top-notch
paella.

**XIAO WANG'S FAMILY
RESTAURANT** 小王府
Chinese Homestyle   Y
☎ 6594 3602; 2 Guanghua Dongli 光
华路东里2号; ⏱ 11am-10.30pm;
🚇 Guomao
A long-time favourite with
Beijingers, Xiao Wang's extensive

menu will satisfy most tastes. The
deep-fried spare ribs and hot-and-
spicy Xinjiang chicken wings are
classics. They do a lean and tasty
Peking duck here too. English
menu.

🍸 DRINK

CENTRO 炫酷 *Lounge*
☎ 6561 8833, ext 42; Kerry Center
Hotel, 1 Guanghua Lu 光华路1号,
嘉里中心饭店; ⏱ 24hr;
🚇 Guomao
A swish place featuring a glossy
black bar to sit at and lots of
inviting sofas to sink into, Centro
attracts business types and those
out to impress their dates. Cool
cocktails and live jazz, as well
as DJs on the weekend, keep it
jumping.

LAN 兰会所 *Lounge, Club*
☎ 5109 6012; 4th fl, LG Twin Towers
Shopping Mall B-12, Jianguomenwai
Dajie 建国门外大街乙12号双
子座大厦4层; ⏱ 11am-2am;
🚇 Yonganli
You'll find paintings that dangle
from the ceiling, giant mirrors
against the walls, fin-de-siècle-
style furniture, as well as the
most extravagant toilets in the
city. They all make this Philippe
Starck–designed bar by far Beijing's most eye-catching nightlife
destination. Beijing's movers and
shakers gather here.

DISTRICTS

SOUTH CHAOYANG

Y STONE BOAT BAR 石舫酒吧
Bar, Cafe
☎ 6501 9986; southwest corner, Ritan Park 日坛公园西南角; ⏱ 10am-late;
Ⓜ Jianguomen

A lovely, low-key bar, at its best on a summer evening, the Stone Boat has mellow live music and an outside area where you can sip your drink beneath the trees of Ritan Park. During the day, it's an equally pleasant cafe. To get here after the park shuts, tell the guards at the south gate where you're going and they'll let you in.

★ PLAY

☆ GT BANANA 吧那那 *Club*
☎ 6526 3939; SciTech Hotel, 22 Jianguomenwai Dajie 建国门外大街 22号赛特饭店; cover charge Y30-50;
⏱ 8.30pm-4am Sun-Thu, to 5am Fri & Sat; Ⓜ Jianguomen or Yonganli

Highly popular with the locals, Banana has one of the biggest dance floors in town and the DJs keep it packed with a no-nonsense mix of happy house and techno. There's an upstairs lounge area where foreign DJs sometimes play a more eclectic mix of sounds.

>XUANWU 宣武

Southwest of Tiananmen Sq, Xuanwu is a souvenir hunter's paradise. It's home to the bustling and historic Dazhalan Jie, where many of Beijing's oldest shops can be found, and the charming Liulichang Xijie, the place to head to for calligraphy and traditional art, as well as antiques and Mao-era memorabilia.

But there's more to Xuanwu than just shopping. Despite some serious redevelopment, there are still plenty of *hutong* (alleyways) running through it, while this is also where you'll find theatres staging Peking opera and acrobatics. In the south of Xuanwu is Niu Jie, the centre of Beijing's Muslim community, as well as Fayuan Temple, an ancient and important Buddhist shrine.

The western end of Dazhalan Jie was undergoing a major makeover at the time of writing, so expect some changes. Subway line 4 runs north–south through Xuanwu, but otherwise you'll have to rely on taxis to get around.

XUANWU

🅲 SEE
Beijing Museum of Red
Chamber Culture &
Art 1 A5
Fayuan Temple 2 B4
Niujie Mosque 3 B3

🅰 SHOP
Maliandao Tea Market ...4 A3
Rongbaozhai 5 C2

Ruifuxiang 6 D2
Tongrentang 7 D2
Yuehaixuan
Musical Instrument
Store 8 C2

🍴 EAT
Goubuli 9 D2
Turpan
Restaurant 10 B3

⭐ PLAY
Huguang Guild
Hall 11 C3
Lao She Tea
House 12 D2
Tianqiao Acrobatics
Theatre 13 D4

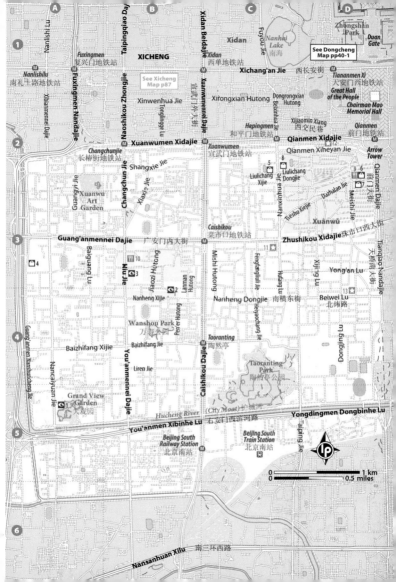

👁 SEE

👁 BEIJING MUSEUM OF RED CHAMBER CULTURE & ART
北京红楼文化艺术博物馆

☎ 6354 4993; 12 Nancaiyuan Jie 南菜园街12号; admission Y40; ⏱ 7.30am-6pm Apr-Oct, to 5pm Nov-Mar; 🚇 Beijing South Railway Station

A tranquil oasis in busy Xuanwu, this is a replica of the garden in Cao Xueqin's classic Chinese novel *Dream of the Red Mansion*. Cryptic English signs explain key points in the story. It's sometimes called the Grand View Garden.

👁 FAYUAN TEMPLE 法源寺

☎ 6353 3966; 7 Fayuansi Qianjie 法源寺前街7号; admission Y5; ⏱ 8.30am-4pm; 🚇 Caishikou or Taoranting

Home to the China Buddhism College, this temple was established in the 7th century and buzzes with worshippers and student monks. Be sure to see the recently restored Guanyin Hall, which has several statues of the Goddess of Mercy.

👁 NIUJIE MOSQUE
牛街礼拜寺

☎ 6353 2564; 88 Niu Jie 牛街88号; admission Y10, Muslims free; ⏱ 8am-6pm; 🚇 Caishikou

Beijing's largest and most important mosque dates back to the 10th century and is a fascinating mix of Islamic and Chinese architectural styles. People here are friendly, but dress appropriately and avoid it on Friday, the Muslim holy day.

🛍 SHOP

🛍 RONGBAOZHAI 荣宝斋
Chinese Art

☎ 6303 6090; 19 Liulichang Xijie 琉璃厂西街19号; ⏱ 9am-5.30pm; 🚇 Hepingmen

Calligraphy, prints and scroll paintings, as well as paper, ink and brushes, are on offer at this state-run establishment. You can sometimes be given a 10% discount here.

🛍 RUIFUXIANG
瑞蚨祥丝绸店 *Silk*

☎ 6303 5313; 5 Dazhalan Jie 大栅栏街5号; ⏱ 9.30am-9pm; 🚇 Qianmen

One of the best places in town to hunt for silk; there's an incredible selection of Shandong fabric here. It also sells ready-made, traditional Chinese clothing on the 2nd floor.

🛍 TONGRENTANG 同仁堂
Chinese Herbal Medicine

☎ 6303 1155; 34 Dazhalan Jie 大栅栏街34号; ⏱ 8am-7.30pm; 🚇 Qianmen

Peddling pills and potions since 1669, this was the former royal dispensary. Now, it claims to be able to cure anything from fright to

Wang Lin Peng
Director of the Acupuncture Department at the Beijing Traditional Chinese Medicine Hospital

Why did you choose to become a Traditional Chinese Medicine (TCM) doctor? I wanted to be a doctor; it was my college in Beijing that thought I was more suited to TCM than Western medicine. **How different is TCM to Western medicine?** It's very different. Western medicine is based on science. TCM is based on thousands of years of experience and philosophy. **Are you surprised that TCM is now popular in the West?** No, Westerners see the value of TCM in treating certain illnesses. If you have insomnia, a Western doctor will prescribe sleeping pills. But we'll look for the underlying reasons why you're not sleeping and then use acupuncture to resolve that. **Do you use TCM when you're ill?** Absolutely. I'd never go to Western medicine hospitals unless I had a very specific illness, like heart disease, which we don't treat here.

encephalitis. Traditional Chinese Medicine doctors are available for on-the-spot consultations.

☐ YUEHAIXUAN MUSICAL INSTRUMENT STORE
乐海轩门市部 Souvenirs

☎ 6303 1472; 97 Liulichang Dongjie 琉璃厂东街97号; ⏱ 9.30am-6.30pm; Ⓜ Hepingmen

Friendly shop specialising in traditional Chinese instruments, such as the zither-like guzheng. It stocks many esoteric instruments from Tibet and Mongolia too.

🍴 EAT

🍴 GOUBULI 狗不理 Chinese Dumplings   Y

☎ 6303 2280; 31 Dazhalan Jie 大栅栏街31号; ⏱ 7.30am-midnight; Ⓜ Qianmen

---

ALL THE TEA IN CHINA

South of Beijing West Railway Station is Maliandao, the largest tea market in northern China. Although it doesn't have all the tea in China, there's an awful lot of it here and most vendors are happy to let you taste some of their brews. Maliandao Lu itself has loads of tea shops, where you can pick up tea sets and tea at cheaper prices than you'll find in the stores in tourist areas. To get here, take the subway to Junshibowuguan and then a taxi.

The Beijing outlet of a famous Tianjin restaurant, Goubuli is packed throughout the day with people munching on the baozi (meat- or vegetable-filled steamed buns) that are the house specialty. Picture menu is available.

🍴 TURPAN RESTAURANT
吐鲁番餐厅 Chinese Muslim   Y

☎ 8316 4691; 6 Niu Jie 牛街6号; ⏱ 11am-9pm; Ⓜ Caishikou; ✕

This cavernous place is the local population's most popular Muslim eatery on Nui Jie. The helpful staff will guide you through the extensive picture menu of dishes from the mainly Muslim, far-western province of Xinjiang. The lamb kebabs (羊肉串) are a must try.

⭐ PLAY

☆ HUGUANG GUILD HALL
湖广会馆 Peking Opera

☎ 6351 8284; www.beijinghuguang.com; 3 Hufang Lu 虎坊路3号; tickets Y180-680; ⏱ 7.30pm; Ⓜ Caishikou

With its magnificent interior, the historic Huguang (built in 1807) is a great place to enjoy your first Peking opera. Earphones are available (Y30) to translate performances into English or Japanese.

☆ LAO SHE TEA HOUSE

老舍茶馆 *Peking Opera, Live Music*

☎ 6303 6830; www.laosheteahouse .com, in Chinese; 3 Qianmen Xidajie 前门 西大街3号; **evening tickets Y180-380;** ⏱ **7.50pm;** Ⓜ **Qianmen**

The 3rd-floor theatre has nightly shows of Peking opera or Chinese folk music, and sometimes stages magic and acrobatics performances. There are also daily shadow-puppet shows, usually from 6pm to 7pm, in the tea house.

☆ TIANQIAO ACROBATICS THEATRE

天桥杂技剧场 *Acrobatics*

☎ 6303 7449; 95 Tianqiao Shichang Jie 天桥市场街95号; **tickets Y180-380;** ⏱ **5.30pm & 7.15pm;** Ⓜ **Qianmen or Caishikou**

Terrific acrobatics shows are staged at this intimate, 100-year-old theatre. Make sure you don't end up in the Tianqiao Theatre, which hosts domestic and foreign dance companies and singers, across from here on Beiwei Lu.

>XICHENG 西城

Xicheng, like its neighbour Dongcheng, was originally inside Beijing's city walls, where the elite of the old imperial city lived. Consequently, it's packed with sights and *hutong* (alleyways). Now, though, it's most notable for the interconnected lakes that sit in the middle of the district. They provide Beijingers with hours of open-air fun, whether it's ice skating in the winter or messing around on boats in the summer.

The district has also moved with the times. It has some of the most intriguing new additions to the Beijing skyline, including the Capital Museum and the controversial National Grand Theatre, while the Xidan area is a huge shopping zone. Best of all, the lakes of Shichahai have become one of the city's nightlife hubs (see the boxed text, p88) and their shores are jammed with restaurants and bars that are especially popular with the locals.

Transport is a breeze in Xicheng, thanks to subway lines 1, 2, 4 and 13, which all criss-cross the district.

XICHENG

👁 SEE
Beihai Park **1** D4
Capital Museum **2** A5
Great Hall of the
    People **3** D5
Jingshan Park **4** D4
Mei Lanfang Former
    Residence **5** C3
Miaoying Temple White
    Dagoba **6** C4
Prince Gong's
    Residence **7** D3

🛍 SHOP
Xing Mu's Handicrafts ...**8** D3

🍴 EAT
Café Sambal **9** D2
Han Cang **10** D3
Hutong Pizza **11** D3
Le Petit Saigon **12** D2
Yuelu Shanwu **13** D3

🍸 DRINK
Bed Bar **14** D2
La Baie des Anges ...... (see 11)
No Name Bar **15** D3

⭐ PLAY
National Centre for the
    Performing Arts **16** D5
What? Bar **17** D4

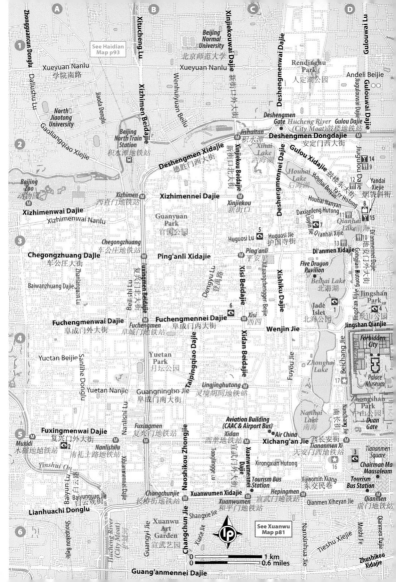

SEE

BEIHAI PARK 北海公园

☎ 6403 1102; Wenjin Jie 文津街; admission Y10; ⏱ 6am-8pm, sights 9am-5pm, last entry 4pm; ⊕ Xisi

Dominated by its huge lake and the White Dagoba that sits on an island in the middle of it, Beihai mixes culture – temples and pavilions to explore – with the chance to laze the day away on a pedalo (Y40, Y200 deposit). You can also enter the park from the north gate on Di'anmen Xidajie (Map p87, D3).

CAPITAL MUSEUM 首都博物馆

☎ 6337 0491; www.capitalmuseum.org .cn; 16 Fuxingmenwai Dajie 复兴门外大街16号; admission Y30; ⏱ 9am-5pm Tue-Sun, last entry 4pm; ⊕ Muxidi

Opened in 2006 to much acclaim, the Capital Museum has raised the bar for every cultural institution in town, thanks to both its thoughtful presentation of some very impressive exhibits and the showcase building (see p20) housing them. The galleries track the evolution of Beijing, as well as highlighting major Chinese cultural achievements. There are displays of porcelain, jade and Buddhist statues, but be sure to visit the fascinating gallery devoted to Beijing folk customs. An audio-guide is Y30 with a Y100 deposit.

HOUHAI

The three lakes that make up the Shichahai area are collectively known to Beijingers as Houhai, and are a great place to see the locals at play. In summer especially, Houhai is one of the most popular night-time destinations in the city. Pedalos jostle for space on the lakes, and young Beijingers crowd out the bars and restaurants that line the shores. Meanwhile, the older generation indulges in some sedate ballroom dancing or lounges shore side gossiping. Houhai is pretty busy in the winter too, when the lakes freeze over and they become the best place in Beijing to ice skate.

GREAT HALL OF THE PEOPLE 人民大会堂

☎ 6309 6935; Tiananmen Sq 天安门广场; admission Y30; ⏱ 8.30am-4.30pm, last entry 4pm; ⊕ Tiananmen Xi

Home of the National People's Congress, this intimidating, Stalinist-style colossus is open to the public when the Congress isn't sitting or the bigwigs aren't welcoming foreign heads of state. The compulsory bag check is Y2 to Y5. For more on Tiananmen Sq, see p12.

JINGSHAN PARK 景山公园

☎ 6403 8098; Jingshan Qianjie 景山前街; admission Y2; ⏱ 6am-9.30pm; ⊕ Dongsi

Climb the hill here, made from earth excavated to construct the nearby Forbidden City's moat, for spectacular, memorable views across the rooftops of the palace and on to Tiananmen Sq (p12).

◉ MEI LANFANG FORMER RESIDENCE 梅兰芳纪念馆
☎ 6618 0351; www.meilanfang.com.cn; 9 Huguosi Lu 护国寺路9号; admission Y10; ⏰ 9am-4pm Tue-Sun Apr-Nov; ◉ Ping'anli

The most iconic Peking opera performer of all, Mei Lanfang (1894–1961) was famous for playing female roles and popularising Peking opera (p23) in the West. This museum in his former home shows his costumes and photos of him performing. English captions.

◉ MIAOYING TEMPLE WHITE DAGOBA 妙应寺白塔
☎ 6616 0211; 171 Fuchengmennei Dajie 阜成门内大街171号; admission Y20; ⏰ 9am-4pm Tue-Sun; ◉ Xisi

The largest surviving Yuan-dynasty monument in Beijing (1206–1368), the chalk-white pagoda here makes a great landmark. There are hundreds of Tibetan Buddhist statues too. After visiting, plunge into the surrounding alleyways for a taste of the local *hutong* life.

◉ PRINCE GONG'S RESIDENCE 恭王府
☎ 6616 5005; 14 Liuyin Jie 柳荫街14号; admission Y40; ⏰ 8.30am-4.30pm; ◉ Ping'anli

One of Beijing's largest residential compounds, this elaborately restored collection of pavilions has fantastic gardens. But it heaves with domestic tour groups, so get here early to avoid the crowds. From March to October, **Peking opera** (☎ 6618 6628; tickets Y80-120; ⏰ 7.30-8.40pm) performances are staged here too.

🛍 SHOP
🛍 XING MU'S HANDICRAFTS 兴木手工 *Souvenirs*
☎ 8402 1831; www.craftxm.com, in Chinese; 2 Yandai Xiejie 烟袋斜街2号; ⏰ 10am-midnight; ◉ Gulou Dajie

The hand-bound books, some made of hemp and linen and emblazoned with Peking opera masks and scenes of Beijing life, make ideal gifts, or a good diary to record your Beijing trip. The shelves are also loaded down with sheaves of artisan paper.

🍴 EAT
🍴 CAFÉ SAMBAL
Southeast Asian   YY
☎ 6400 4875; 43 Doufuchi Hutong 旧鼓楼大街豆腐池胡同43号; ⏰ 11am-midnight; ◉ Gulou Dajie; Ⓥ

Housed in a cool, converted courtyard house just off Jiugulou Dajie (Map p87, D2), come here for classic Malaysian cuisine – curries, beef rendang and sambals – as well as for potent mojitos.

🍴 HAN CANG 汉仓 Hakka Y
☎ 6404 2259; 12 Qianhai Nanyan 前海南沿 12号; ⏱ 11am-10.30pm; Ⓜ Ping'anli

You can eat lakeside in the summer at this deservedly popular Houhai (see the boxed text, p88) hang-out. Hakka cuisine uses a lot of fresh fish: try the fried fish in pine nuts, or the prawns in a bucket of salt, but there's a huge range of options here. English menu.

🍴 HUTONG PIZZA 胡同比萨 Pizza Y
☎ 8322 8916; 9 Yindingqiao Hutong 银锭桥胡同 9号; ⏱ 11am-10.30pm; Ⓜ Gulou Dajie; Ⓥ

Hard to find – it's down a hutong off Houhai (see the boxed text, p88) – but make the effort because the trademark square, and very large, pizzas here are the best in town. There are tons of options to choose from, or build your own. Good vegie burgers too. Book ahead at peak hours.

🍴 LE PETIT SAIGON 西贡在巴黎 French, Vietnamese Y
☎ 6401 8465; 141 Jiugulou Dajie 旧鼓楼大街 141号; ⏱ 11.30am-midnight; Ⓜ Gulou Dajie

The Little Saigon is a stylish bistro, with a menu that mixes classic Vietnamese, like pho and lemon chicken, and French dishes to decent effect. The desserts are especially good. There's a strong wine list and proper coffee, which you can enjoy on the roof terrace in the summer.

🍴 YUELU SHANWU 岳麓山屋 Hunan Y
☎ 6617 2696; 19a Qianhai Xiyan 前海西沿甲19号; ⏱ 11am-11pm; Ⓜ Gulou Dajie

This two-storey place has a marvellous view over Houhai (see the boxed text, p88), while the catalogue-sized English picture menu is heavy on the searing, spicy flavours of Hunan province. But not every dish will take the lining off your mouth; try the home-style pork or the boiled frog.

🍸 DRINK
🍸 BED BAR 床吧 Bar
☎ 8400 1554; 17 Zhangwang Hutong, Jiugulou Dajie 旧鼓楼大街张旺胡同 17号; ⏱ 4pm-2am Mon & Tue, noon-late Wed-Sun; Ⓜ Gulou Dajie

A wicked layout of interconnected rooms and traditional Chinese beds make Bed a great spot; even if it's crowded, and it often is, there's normally somewhere to hide away if you want. There are

DJs at the weekend and proper mixed drinks too. There's a sign at the entrance of the alley to guide you there.

▼ LA BAIE DES ANGES
天使港湾法国休闲酒吧 *Bar*

☎ 6657 1605; 5 Nanguanfang Hutong 后海南官房胡同 5号; ⏱ 6pm-2am summer, 7pm-2am winter Tue-Sun; ⊕ Gulou Dajie

Lovers of the grape make tracks for this cool bar a few doors down from Hutong Pizza (opposite). French-run, it has weekly wine specials, as well as a huge selection of vintages to choose from. There's normally live music on Friday and Saturday.

▼ NO NAME BAR 无名酒吧
Cafe, Bar

☎ 6401 8541; 3 Qianhai Dongyan 前海东沿 3号; ⏱ noon-2am; ⊕ Gulou Dajie

The first, and still the best, of the bars that have sprung up around Houhai's shores (see the boxed text, p88), the No Name is an easygoing, mellow joint, where you can sit in a rattan armchair and watch the world pass you by through the large windows.

★ PLAY

★ NATIONAL CENTRE FOR THE PERFORMING ARTS
国家大剧院 *Theatre*

☎ 6655 0000; www.chncpa.org; 2 Xichang'an Jie 西长安街 2号; tickets Y80-880; ⊕ Tiananmen Xi

One of the jewels in Beijing's architectural crown (see p20), this colossal, dome-shaped venue is *the* place to listen to classical music, from China and abroad, as well as to watch ballet, opera and Chinese classical dance. It's sometimes known as the National Grand Theatre. Check the website for the schedule.

★ WHAT? BAR 什么?酒吧
Live Music

☎ 133 4112 2757; 72 Beichang Jie 北长街 72号; cover charge Y30; ⏱ 3pm-midnight; ⊕ Tiananmen Xi

A tiny club, with a shoebox-sized stage, that has loads of character and is a great place to check out up-and-coming local talent. Gigs are on Friday and Saturday, and the cover charge includes a free beer. It's just north of the west gate of the Forbidden City.

>HAIDIAN 海淀

Occupying a vast swath of west and northwest Beijing, Haidian is a district of huge contrasts. There are important historical sites like the stunning Summer Palace, as well as museums and temples galore. And if that wasn't enough, Haidian has the capital's biggest parks, where you can escape the city.

The Summer Palace is the highlight of the district, and it's possible to travel there by boat along the canal that cuts through Haidian. But there's also the botanical gardens and zoo, or you can head to the Fragrant Hills and roam the former hunting grounds of the imperial family. In the south of Haidian, the Weigongcun area has some of the capital's finest ethnic minority restaurants.

Also home to most of Beijing's universities, Haidian is now well served by subway lines. Line 13 swoops up from the east, while line 10 heads west–east through the heart of Haidian. Line 4 runs north–south through the west of the district, linking the Summer Palace with the south of Haidian.

HAIDIAN

📷 SEE
Beijing Zoo **1** C4
Wuta Temple **2** C3

🍽 EAT
Golden Peacock **3** B3

⭐ PLAY
National Library
Concert Hall **4** B3

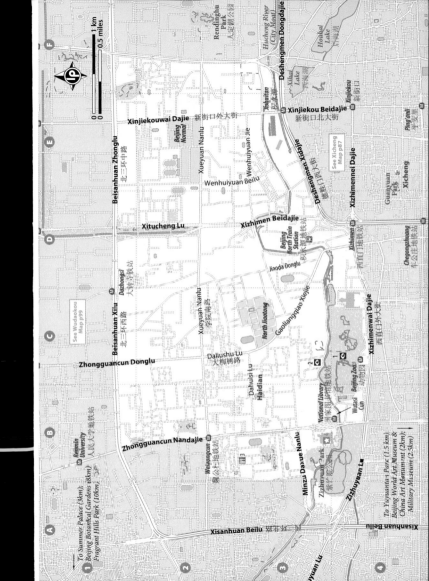

Xinjiekouwai Dajie 新街口外大街

Beisanhuan Zhonglu 北三环中路

Beijing Normal

Xueyuan Nanlu

Xitucheng Lu

Wenhuiyuan Jie

Wenhuiyuan Beilu

Xinjiekou Beidajie 新街口北大街

Deshengmen Dongdajie

Rendinghu Park 人定湖公园

Hucheng River (City Moat)

Xihai Lake 西海

Houhai Lake 后海湖

Xinjiekou 新街口

Ping'anli 平安里

Deshengmen-Xidajie 德胜门西大街

See Xicheng Map p87

Xizhimennei Dajie

Xizhimen Beidajie

Beijing North Train Station 北京北站地铁站

Jianda Donglu

Guanyuan Park 官园 Xicheng

Chegongzhuang 车公庄地铁站

Beisanhuan Xilu 北三环西路

Dahongsi 大钟寺铁路

Xueyuan Nanlu 学院南路

North Jiaotong

Gaoliangqiao Xiejie 高粱桥斜街

See Wudaokou Map p99

Zhongguancun Donglu

Daliushu Lu 大柳树路

Dahuisi lu Haidian

National Library 国家图书馆地铁站

Wutasi Cun

Beijing Zoo 动物园

Xizhimenwai Dajie 西直门外大街

Zhongguancun Nandajie

Renmin University 人民大学地铁站

Weigongcun 魏公村地铁站

Zizhuyuan Park 紫竹院

Minzu Da-xue Nanlu

Zizhuyuan Lu

To Yuyuantan Park (1.5km); Beijing World Art Museum & China Art Monument (2km); Military Museum (2.5km)

Xisanhuan Beilu 西三环北路

Xisanhuan Beilu

To Summer Palace (3km); Beijing Botanical Gardens (8km); Fragrant Hills Park (10km)

1 km
0.5 miles

N

A B C D E F
1 2 3 4

👁 SEE

👁 BEIJING BOTANIC GARDENS
北京植物园
☎ 6259 1283; Wofusi Lu
卧佛寺路; admission Y5;
🕐 7am-5pm; 🚇 Anheqiaobei,
then taxi

With the Western Hills in the background, these gardens are a fine place to commune with nature. There are plenty of paths to follow, while the **Conservatory** (admission Y50; 🕐 8.30am-4pm) overflows with 3000 types of plants. Amidst the flora is the **Sleeping Buddha Temple** (admission Y5; 🕐 8am-5pm), which has a vast effigy of the Sakyamuni Buddha.

👁 BEIJING WORLD ART MUSEUM & CHINA MILLENNIUM MONUMENT
中华世纪坛世界艺术馆
☎ 5980 2222; www.worldartmuseum
.com; 9a Fuxing Lu 复兴路甲9号;
admission Y30; 🕐 9am-6pm, last entry
5pm; 🚇 Junshibowuguan

Housed in the bombastic China Millennium Monument, the World Art Museum hosts excellent temporary exhibitions that run the gamut of ancient art to modern design and avant-garde photography. A ticket to the monument, which is shaped like a giant sundial, gets you into the museum as well.

Detail showing some of the intricate work on the Hall of Benevolence and Longevity, Summer Palace

WORTH THE TRIP – THE SUMMER PALACE

The **Summer Palace** (颐和园; ☎ 6288 1144; Yiheyuan Lu 颐和园路; 1 Apr-31 Oct Y60, 1 Nov-31 Mar Y50; 🕙 8.30am-5pm; 🚇 Xiyuan) was the pleasure palace of Emperor Qianlong (1711–99), see p14.

Just inside the East Gate is the chief palace structure, the **Hall of Benevolence and Longevity**, where the emperor handled state affairs and received envoys.

Nearby, the **Garden of Virtue and Harmony** comprises two halls and a theatre stage. The stage is where the imperial family watched Peking opera, a favourite of Empress Cixi. From May through August it hosts free performances (usually acrobatics or traditional dance) hourly from 9am to 4pm. Theatrical costumes and props are displayed in the neighbouring pavilions.

The **Long Corridor**, a 728m pavilion decorated with mythical scenes, is west of here. **Longevity Hill** looms to the north and has most of the palace's grand halls and temples. Further on is Cixi's infamous **marble boat**, which became a symbol of the imperial family's extravagance, and the ferry (Y8) that crosses to South Lake Island.

South Lake Island's **Hall of Embracing the Universe** contains a small exhibition on Puyi, the last emperor. From here, go south to the **Western Corridor** (see the boxed text, p15) or north to the **Wenchang Gallery**, which houses Qing artefacts, as well as jade and porcelain.

To get to the palace by boat, see p145. Admission to the grounds only is Y20. An audio-guide is Y40.

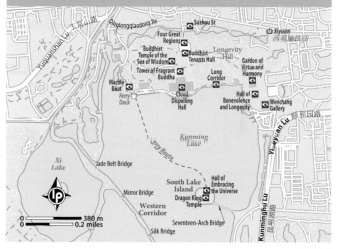

⊙ BEIJING ZOO 北京动物园

☎ 6831 4411; 137 Xizhimenwai Dajie 西直门外大街137号; admission Y15, panda house Y5; ⏲ 7.30am-7pm; ⊕ Beijing Zoo

The only place where you'll get to see pandas in the capital, Beijing's zoo has upped its game recently, even if some of the enclosures will make animal lovers wince. Located in what used to be the garden of a Qing-era worthy, it's a nice spot for a walk. The more modern aquarium at the back of the complex has fun seal and dolphin shows. You can also catch a boat to the Summer Palace from here (p145).

⊙ FRAGRANT HILLS PARK 香山公园

☎ 6259 1283; Xiangshan Lu, northwest Beijing 北京西北香山路; admission Y10, temples Y10; ⏲ 6am-6.30pm 1 Apr-30 Jun & 1 Sep- 15 Nov, to 7pm 1 Jul-31 Aug, to 6pm 16 Nov-31 Mar; ⊕ Anheqiaobei, then taxi

Superb in the autumn, when the abundant maple leaves turn a flaming red, but great any time when the weather is right, this park snuggled in the Western Hills teems with hikers and day trippers at weekends. Make sure to check the view of Beijing available from Incense-Burner Peak – there's a chairlift (one-way/return Y30/Y50) if you don't fancy the walk – and to

visit the lovely Azure Clouds Temple (⏲ 8am-5pm), which dates back to the Yuan dynasty.

⊙ MILITARY MUSEUM 军事博物馆

☎ 6686 6244; 9 Fuxing Lu 复兴路9号; admission Y20; ⏲ 8am-5pm, last entry 4pm; ⊕ Junshibowuguan

From the humble swords and rifles of earlier eras, to the tanks and fighter planes of more modern times, as well as surface-to-air missiles, there's enough hardware on display here to start WWIII. But despite the martial tone, this is one of Beijing's more popular museums. The sections on China's many wars are fascinating, although there's a lack of English captions.

⊙ WUTA TEMPLE 五塔寺

☎ 6217 6058; 24 Wutasi Cun 五塔寺村24号; admission Y20; ⏲ 9am-4.30pm Tue-Sun; ⊕ National Library

It looks more like an Indian temple because this secluded, Ming-era Buddhist structure has a unique five-pagoda roof. A very narrow staircase, which is not always open, leads to the roof. At the back of the complex is the interesting Stone Carving Museum, with a collection of stone statues and stelae. The temple is directly opposite the rear exit of the Beijing Zoo (left).

EAT ETHNIC CHINESE CUISINE IN WEIGONGCUN

The area around Weigongcun is a great place to try some of the food eaten by China's 56 ethnic minorities. With the Central University for the Nationalities, China's specialist college for its non-Han Chinese citizens, nearby, a whole restaurant strip catering to the people from the country's most far-flung points has emerged. Now, there are eateries specialising in everything from the Dai cuisine of the southwest (below), to Mongolian, Tibetan and Xinjiang food. All are run by people from those regions, which guarantees not only authenticity but also a steady stream of exiles yearning for a taste of home. But many Beijingers eat here too, drawn by the knowledge that Weigongcun is one of the city's best, but least-known, restaurant streets.

👁 YUYUANTAN PARK
玉渊潭公园

☎ 8865 3804; Yuyuantan Nanlu 玉渊潭南路; admission Y2; ⏱ 6am-10pm, last entry 9pm; 🚇 Junshibowuguan

With a huge body of water divided into east and west lakes, it's a lovely park for walks, especially the short, but pretty west-lake route. In winter, you can ice skate; rent equipment from the vendors who gather around the lakes. Boats to the Summer Palace leave from the Bayi Lake Dock (p145).

🍴 EAT
🍴 GOLDEN PEACOCK
金孔雀德宏傣味餐厅 *Dai* Y

☎ 6893 2030; Weigongcun 魏公村韦伯豪家园南门对面; ⏱ 11am-10pm; 🚇 Weigongcun

Make sure you try the pineapple rice at this unpretentious and popular restaurant (get here early

or book ahead). It specialises in the cuisine of the Dai ethnic minority from southwest China, who use a lot of the flavourings, like lemongrass, common to Southeast Asian cuisine. The rice wine here is a fine tipple.

⭐ PLAY
⭐ NATIONAL LIBRARY CONCERT HALL
国家图书馆音乐厅
Live Music

☎ 6848 5462; 33 Zhongguancun Nandajie 中关村南大街33号; 🚇 National Library

It's not just classical music that you can hear, at this impressive space. Chinese classical dance, an ancient art form that blends elements of martial arts with traditional storytelling, and folk music, both Chinese and foreign, is performed here too, and brings in the crowds.

>WUDAOKOU 五道口

The most happening neighbourhood of Haidian district (p92), Wudaokou has emerged in recent years as a distinct area in its own right, thanks to its thriving bar, club, music and restaurant scene. In particular, the 'Wu' is an essential stop for anyone interested in checking out Beijing's ever-increasing number of bands.

Wudaokou, which means 'five rail crossings', is a young neighbourhood by Beijing's standards, dating back 100 years or so. Its growth was driven by the establishment here of Peking and Qinghua Universities, China's two premier academic institutions. With a number of other colleges also in the area, Wudaokou is Beijing's student central.

If you've spent the day at the nearby Summer Palace, then a night out in Wudaokou makes for a great contrast. There aren't many ancient sights here; rather, it's a place to experience modern Beijing, and there is a plethora of bars, cafes and restaurants to choose from. Most of the action is on or off Chengfu Lu, where subway line 13 will drop you.

WUDAOKOU

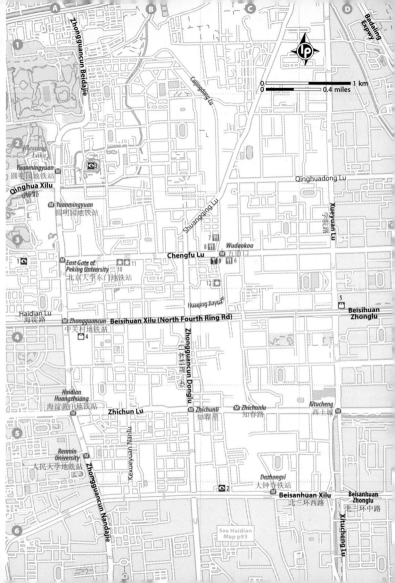

A1 **Zhongguancun Beidajie**

B1 **Badaling Expwy**

C1 **Caijingdong Lu**

A2 Blessing Lake
圆明园地铁站
Yuanmingyuan
圆明园地铁站

A2 **Qinghua Xilu**
清华西路

C2 **Qinghuadong Lu**

B3 **Shuangqing Lu**

D3 **Xueyuan Lu**
学院路

B3 7
B3 **Wudaokou**
Chengfu Lu
B3 9   6

A3 1
East Gate of Peking University
北京大学东门地铁站
11
10
12

A3 **Yuanmingyuan**
圆明园地铁站

C3 **Huaqing Jiayuan**

D3 5
Beisihuan Zhonglu

A4 **Haidian Lu**
海淀路
Zhongguancun
中关村地铁站   4
Beisihuan Xilu (North Fourth Ring Rd)

B4 **Zhongguancun Donglu**
中关村东路

A5 **Haidian Huangzhuang**
海淀黄庄地铁站
Zhichun Lu

B5 **Zhichunli**
知春里
C5 **Zhichunlu**
知春路
C5 **Xitucheng**
西土城

A5 **Kexueyuan Nanlu**
科学院南路

A5 **Renmin University**
人民大学地铁站

A5 **Zhongguancun Nandajie**
中关村南大街

C5 **Dazhongsi**
大钟寺地铁站

B5 2

C5 **Beisanhuan Xilu**
北三环西路

D5 **Beisanhuan Zhonglu**
北三环中路

D5 **Xitucheng Lu**

B6 See Haidian Map p93

DISTRICTS

WUDAOKOU

👁 SEE

🔷 ARTHUR M SACKLER MUSEUM OF ART & ARCHAEOLOGY

赛克勒考古与艺术博物馆

☎ 6275 1667; Peking University 北京大学西门内; admission Y5; ⏱ 9am-4.30pm; 🚇 Yuanmingyuan

Home to an important, well-presented collection of relics from primordial China, including the skeleton of the 280,000-year-old Jinniushan Man, this museum is tucked away on the leafy campus of Peking University. It's a good spot to escape the hustle of Wudaokou. To get here, enter via the west gate of the university and follow the signs.

🔷 GREAT BELL TEMPLE 大钟寺

☎ 6225 0819; 31a Beisanhuan Xilu 北三环西路甲31号; admission Y10; ⏱ 9am-4.30pm; 🚇 Dazhongsi

Ring the bell here and half of Beijing will hear it, because the centrepiece of this temple, which was once where emperors came to pray for rain, is a massive Ming-dynasty bell that weighs in at almost 50 tonnes. There's a huge array of less imposing bells too, all inscribed with delicate characters. There's an audio-guide available

The decorative features of the Great Bell Temple are as glorious as the bells

for Y10, although earplugs might be more suitable.

OLD SUMMER PALACE
圆明园
☎ 6262 8501; www.yuanmingyuan park.com.cn, in Chinese; 28 Qinghua Xilu 清华西路28号; ruins Y25, park Y10; ⏱ 7am-7pm May-Aug, to 6.30pm Sep, Oct & Jan-Mar, to 5.30pm Nov & Dec; ⓜ Yuanmingyuan

Not to be confused with the Summer Palace (see the boxed text, p95), this once glorious complex was sacked by Anglo-French forces in 1860 during the Second Opium War, a humiliation the Chinese have still not forgotten. Although there was a palace here from the 12th century, the buildings destroyed were designed by Jesuit missionaries for Emperor Qianlong (1711–99) in an imitation of a European-style palace. Now, you can wander through the melancholy ruins and then stroll on through the massive park that surrounds them.

Old Summer Palace, magnificent even in ruins

place to come for Beijing's cheapest range of computer software and hardware, cell phones, every type of game and the latest iPods. Not all of it is the real deal, so check what you're buying. But you can bargain here.

WUDAOKOU CLOTHING MARKET 五道口服装市场
Market
☎ 6239 6347; 261 Beisihuan Zhonglu 北四环中路261号; ⏱ 9am-7.30pm; ⓜ Wudaokou

Cool kids head to this two-storey market in their droves, drawn by both the cheap prices and the funky styles which have often been adapted from Korean or Japanese designs. It's at the junction with Xueyuan Lu.

🛍 SHOP
NOVA ZHONGGUANCUN
中关村电子科贸城 *Electronics*
☎ 8253 6688; 18 Zhongguancun Dajie 中关村大街18号; ⏱ 9am-7pm; ⓜ Zhongguancun

Zhongguancun is China's Silicon Valley and this vast mall is the

WUDAOKOU BEER GARDEN

When Beijing emerges from the deep freeze of its winter, so do its residents. Come summer in Wudaokou, the area just west of the subway stop turns into a hugely popular open-air beer garden. Locals and foreigners congregate at the tables, supping draft beers and snacking from the street food stands that surround them. The party starts early here, around 5pm, and continues late, and it gets louder and louder as those Y10 beers disappear down thirsty throats.

🍴 EAT
🍴 GRANDMA'S KITCHEN
祖母的厨房 American   Y
☎ 6266 6105; 5th fl, Wudaokou U-Center, 36 Chengfu Lu 五道口商业中心5层, 成俯路36号; ⌚ 10am-10.30pm; Ⓜ Wudaokou;
If you're craving American-style food, then this homely diner is it. The all-day breakfasts are popular, as are the steaks and burgers, as well as apple pie. It's located on the 5th floor of a busy mall, where there are other eating options, including Vietnamese and Sichuan.

🍴 ISSHIN 日本料理一心 North Asian   Y
☎ 8261 0136; www.isshin.info, in Chinese; 35 Chengfu Lu 成府路35号; Ⓜ Wudaokou

A favourite with locals and expats, Isshin serves affordable sushi and sashimi in cool, dark surroundings, as well as top-notch hotpots and teriyaki dishes. The set lunch is a decent deal. The entrance is just off Shuangqing Lu (双清路) north of Chengfu Lu. Turn left through the big arch.

🍴 SALANG BANG 舍廊旁
Korean   Y
☎ 8261 8201; 3rd fl, Dongyuan Plaza 东源大厦3层; ⌚ 11am-5am; Ⓜ Wudaokou
A big hang-out for the many South Korean students in the area, this slick, spacious and efficient eatery is especially good for Korean barbecue and seafood. All the dishes come with a selection of Korean nibbles like tofu and kimchi.

🍸 DRINK
🍸 LUSH Bar, Cafe
☎ 8286 3566; www.lushbeijing.com; 2nd fl, 1 Huaqing Jiayuan, Chengfu Lu 成府路花清嘉园1号楼2层; ⌚ 24hr; Ⓜ Wudaokou
Whether they're quaffing coffee or slamming beers, Chinese and foreign students camp out here around the clock. Lush also hosts events every night, from movies on Monday and live bands on Friday, to a wildly popular open-mic night on Sunday, making it one of the

Gao Ming
Co-president of the Maybe Mars record label, home to the best of Beijing's indie bands

When did you discover the Beijing music scene? When I went to Peking University, I started listening to a lot of alternative music from the West. Then, around 2004, the Beijing scene just exploded and I started going to see the local bands. **Why are most of the good bands in China from Beijing?** I think Beijing people are more interested in culture than people from other cities. Also, we have more live venues and, most important, there are lots of people who really support the bands. **Do you think the Chinese rock scene will ever become mainstream?** Well, it's already growing fast. In Beijing we're getting high-school students coming to the gigs now. Before, it was always university students. **How different is the Beijing music scene to the West's?** It's not very commercial, which gives the bands a lot of freedom. And Beijing bands are really friendly to each other. I think that's really healthy.

epicentres of Wudaokou life. Happy hour runs from 6pm to 10pm.

⭐ PLAY

⭐ **13 CLUB** 13俱乐部 *Live Music*
☎ 8668 7151; 161 Chengfu Lu 成府路 161号; ⏰ 6pm-late; ⊕ East Gate of Peking University or Wudaokou
Local punk and metal bands are the mainstays here, but other acts also make it onto the stage at this grungy venue down a suitably dark alley. Look for the red sign.

⭐ **D-22** *Live Music*
☎ 6265 3177; www.d22beijing.com; 242 Chengfu Lu 成府路242号; ⏰ 6pm-2am Tue-Sun; ⊕ East Gate of Peking University or Wudaokou

The focal point of the Beijing indie scene, D-22 does a fantastic job of showcasing local bands, and a few foreign ones too. A solid sound system combines with the stripped-down interior to give it the vibe of a London or New York venue. It's a big muso hang-out, so you might find yourself propping up the bar with one of Beijing's guitar heroes.

⭐ **PROPAGANDA** *Club*
☎ 8286 3991; East gate, Huaqing Jiayuan 花清嘉园东门; ⏰ 8pm-late; ⊕ Wudaokou
Loved for its meat-market reputation as much as for its hip-hop soundtrack and cheap drinks, the club is a long-time student favourite and gets packed on weekends.

>HISTORICAL HOTSPOTS

It takes your breath away, the Great Wall of China, seen here at Simatai (p109)

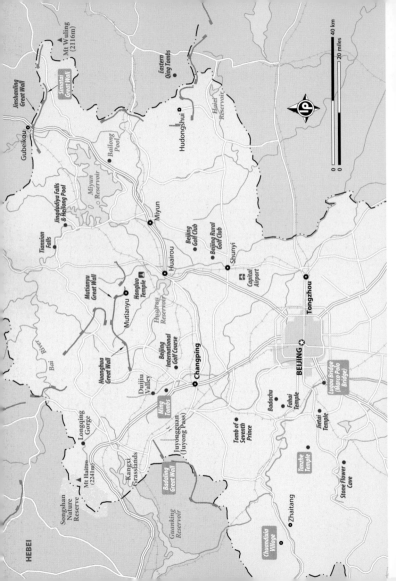

THE GREAT WALL

The very symbol of China, this monument to the country, the Great Wall is an absolute must see. No matter what you've heard about it, or how many pictures you've seen, nothing beats standing on its ramparts and seeing how the wall snakes away along the hills into the far distance.

Meandering its way across China for 8850km, from Xinjiang in the far west to the border with North Korea in the east, the wall is not just an awesome structure but also a very visible reminder of China's turbulent history. It first took shape over 2000 years ago, during the Qin dynasty (221–207 BC), when individual walls scattered across China's northern frontiers were linked to form a mega-wall to keep out sabre-rattling Mongolian nomads.

But when the Qin dynasty fell, the wall began to crumble. Despite efforts over the years to maintain it, it wasn't until 1000 years later that the menacing threat of Genghis Khan and his hordes prompted further construction. Its final incarnation, and the one most visitors see today, came during the Ming dynasty (1368–1644), when the rammed earth used in its original versions was replaced by far more sturdy bricks and stone slabs.

However, the wall didn't stop the Manchus from invading from the northeast to establish the Qing dynasty (1644–1911), just as it failed to keep out Genghis Khan. The wall's great irony is that it rarely stopped enemies but it did work as an elevated highway across mountainous terrain, and its system of watchtowers gave warning of impending attacks.

Much of the Wall has disappeared or is in a state of disrepair. It wasn't until 1984 that it was protected by law and partial restoration was begun.

Depending on the type of experience you want, the Badaling (p108) and Simatai (p109) sections of the wall, both built during the Ming dynasty, are excellent choices for a visit.

COMMUNE BY THE GREAT WALL

For something different, check out **Commune by the Great Wall** (☎ 8118 1888; www .communebythegreatwall.com; Badaling), 70km northwest of Beijing. Stunning contemporary 'villas', each designed differently by some of Asia's hottest architects, form one of the most offbeat and luxurious hotels in Beijing with 46 guest rooms spread among 12 luxury villas. The commune can be experienced on a **guided tour** (per person Y120; 9am-5pm Mon-Thu) through the grounds and any unoccupied rooms. Book the tour in advance.

BADALING GREAT WALL
八达岭长城

Veteran wall walkers might roll their eyes at the mere mention of its name, and it is the attraction at its most touristy, but Badaling still has the classic vista of the wall snaking off into the distance, and the surrounding scenery is striking. Best of all, it's the part of the structure closest to Beijing, so those with limited time can see it on a half-day trip.

Badaling has undergone major renovations, as befits the section of the wall that visiting foreign dignitaries get taken to. It's also overrun with hawkers, snack stands and endless tour groups. But the repairs mean that it's rather safer than more 'wild' strips of the wall, so if you're unable, or unwilling, to traverse very steep inclines, come here.

One way of avoiding the crowds is to visit in the winter, when the snow on the ramparts is extremely photogenic. Wrap up very warm, though, unless you want to return to Beijing with frostbite. In the summer, come on a weekday, or be prepared for suffocating numbers of people.

Cable cars (Y50 round trip) are available to whip you up and down, while the entrance fee also includes admission into the **China Great Wall Museum** (⏰ 9am-4pm).

INFORMATION
Location 70km northwest of Beijing.
Getting there Take the tour bus (see p146).
Contact Call ☎ 6912 1737.
Costs Admission is Y45; an audio-guide is Y40 with a Y100 deposit.
When to go Badaling is open 6am to 8pm in the summer, 7am to 6pm in the winter.

SIMATAI GREAT WALL
司马台长城

With its dizzying descents and very steep climbs, the wall at Simatai is a rugged, sometimes precarious, but always rewarding experience. The scenery is truly dramatic, with watchtowers scattered along the whole stretch here. But you need to be fit and to wear sturdy shoes with a decent grip, while a backpack (daypack) is essential because you'll need your arms free for climbing in places.

Take the **cable car** (1-way/round-trip Y30/50; 🕐 8.30am-4.30pm) up, which takes 15 minutes, followed by the so-called **mini-train** (1-way/round-trip Y20/30), a five-minute ride in what is actually an open funicular.

After that, the wall is a 10-minute walk away. From this point, the wall undulates downhill towards the parking lot. Most people take two to three hours to walk this section. At the end, either walk downhill (20 to 30 minutes) or take the **zip line** (Y35, 3min) over the river to get to the exit. Alternatively, cross the bridge (Y5) and remount the wall for more exploring.

It's a good idea to bring your own water with you; it's far more expensive on the wall here than usual. Food is in short supply, so bring some snacks too.

INFORMATION
Location 110km northeast of Beijing.
Getting there Take the tour bus (see p146).
Contact Call ☎ 6903 1051, or go to www.simatai-greatwall.net (in Chinese).
Costs Admission is Y40.
When to go Simatai is open 8am to 5pm.

MING TOMBS
明十三陵

The final resting place of 13 of the 16 Ming emperors, this imperial grave-yard can be visited on a tour that also incorporates the Badaling section of the Great Wall (p108). In truth, it's the best way to come here because, for all the history surrounding the place, the tombs themselves are not that impressive visually.

When Ming emperors shuffled off this mortal coil, they did it in style. The pomp and ceremony involved the huge burial party travelling to the tombs via the **Spirit Way**, the most beguiling part of any visit here. The 7km stretch of road is lined with stone statues of animals and court officials. Every other animal is in the crouching position and is said to rise at mid-night during the 'changing of the guard'.

Three of the tombs are currently open to the public. The most impos-ing is **Chang Ling**, the resting place of Emperor Yongle. You approach the actual burial mound, which can't be entered, via a series of intricately decorated halls. **Ding Ling**, where Emperor Wan Li is buried, is the only tomb visitors can actually access, via stairs that lead to the underground vault. The other tomb open is **Zhao Ling**, the grave of Emperor Longqing, which sees far fewer visitors than the other two.

A good guide can help bring a visit here alive – it is after all a graveyard – so if you're really interested consider joining an English-language tour (see p153). Be aware too, that group tours never take in all the tombs and usually stop at only one or two of the four sights mentioned above (usually Ding Ling and the Spirit Way).

INFORMATION
Location 50km north of Beijing.
Getting there Take the tour bus (see p146), or bus 345 from Deshengmen (德胜门; Y6, one hour) to Changping Beizan (昌平北站), then bus 314 (Y2) or taxi (Y20).
Contact Call ☎ 6076 1424.
Costs Ding Ling admission is Y65, Chang Ling is Y45 and Zhao Ling is Y30.
When to go The tombs are open from 8.30am to 5.30pm.

LUGOU BRIDGE (MARCO POLO BRIDGE) 卢沟桥

On the far southwestern outskirts of Beijing, the Lugou Bridge dates back to 1189 and is the city's oldest marble bridge. Spanning 266m across the Yongding River, it's most notable for the almost 500 small stone lions that decorate it. Each one is unique, they all have subtle differences, and local folklore insists that they like to move around at night.

The bridge gets its second name because Marco Polo mentioned it in his journals. To the Chinese, though, the bridge is better known for the fact that it was where the first shots of the Sino-Japanese War (1937–45) were fired. After Japanese soldiers illegally occupied a nearby railway junction, Chinese troops retaliated by opening fire on them, which gave Japan a pretext for attacking and then occupying Beijing.

Nearby, the Memorial Hall of the War of Resistance Against Japan offers a harrowing look back at the war. Plenty of photos, but no English captions.

INFORMATION
Location 17km southwest of Beijing.
Getting there Take bus 301 from Qianmen (Y1, one hour) or a taxi.
Contact Call ☎ 8389 4614.
Costs Admission is Y20.
When to go The bridge is open from 8am to 5pm.

HISTORICAL HOTSPOTS

TANZHE TEMPLE
潭柘寺

Beijing's oldest temple is set against the picturesque backdrop of the Western Hills. It's a popular excursion for Beijingers in April, when the magnolias are in bloom, but it's equally impressive at other times of the year, thanks to the way the complex sprawls up a hillside and is surrounded by ancient and gnarly cypress and pine trees that provide some shade.

The temple was built during the Jin dynasty (AD 265–420), although most of the buildings go back only as far as the Ming and Qing dynasties. The main structure is the **Mahavira Hall**, where monks still perform ceremonies. You can also check out the gory fate of hell-bound mortals at the **Dizang Hall**, visit the smoky **Guanyin Cave** where you can taste spring-water tea, or stroke the hanging **Stone Fish** for luck.

About 10km southeast of Tanzhe is the smaller but almost as venerable **Jietai Temple**, which dates back to the 7th century.

INFORMATION
Location The temple is in Mentougou district (门头沟区), 45km west of Beijing.
Getting there Take the subway to Pingguoyuan, then bus 931 (Y3, one hour, every 30 to 40 minutes 6.50am to 5.35pm); note that the last bus from Tanzhe Temple to the subway leaves at 5pm. A taxi is Y30 to Y40 one way.
Contact Call ☎ 6086 2505.
Costs Admission is Y55.
When to go Tanzhe is open from 8am to 5pm.

CHUANDIXIA VILLAGE
川底下村

A visit to this cluster of historic courtyards in a Ming-dynasty village makes a great day trip from Beijing and is a real step back into the past, thanks to the ancient alleyways you can wander down, the 70-odd traditional homes and the beautiful backdrop of terraced orchards and fields rising up the hillside behind the village.

But Chuandixia also has a foot in a more modern time. Maoist slogans from the Cultural Revolution are stencilled throughout the village, and seeing faded exhortations like 'Arm our Minds with Mao Zedong Thought' and 'Proletariats of the World Unite' in such an old-world setting makes for a bizarre juxtaposition of eras.

Chuandixia's relatively isolated location helped it preserve its character long after other villages went down the route of tacking on ugly, brick-built extensions to aged courtyards. The locals have done a good job of preserving the charms of the place, not least because they are well aware of Chuandixia's value as both a location for period TV shows and as a tourist centre.

That means that, should you be stuck here for the night, you won't have a problem finding a place to stay or a restaurant to eat in. But, as the village is small, most people choose to head back to Beijing after a few hours.

INFORMATION

Location 90km west of Beijing.

Getting there From Pingguoyuan subway station there are two daily direct buses (Y10, 7.30am and 12.30pm, returning at 10.30am and 3.30pm). Otherwise, take bus 929 (branch line 支线) to Zhaitang (斋堂; Y8, two hours), then a taxi van (Y20, 15 to 20 minutes). The last bus from Zhaitang to Pingguoyuan leaves at 4.20pm. A return trip by the taxis that will be waiting for you at Pingguoyuan is Y150 to Y200. Some hostels run tours here, as does the China Culture Center (p149).

Contact Call ☎ 6981 9333 or go to www.cuandixia.com.

Costs Admission is Y20.

When to go The ticket office is open from 9am to 6pm.

>SNAPSHOTS

Beijing changes so much and so frequently that it can be a tough town in which to hit the ground running. If your time in the city is limited, then this section will help you identify the best of Beijing. Whether you're after nightlife or temples, you'll find it here.

Shoppers get a high at Sun Dong An Plaza, Wangfujing Dajie (p126)

V

SNAPSHOTS

ACCOMMODATION

Hosting the 2008 Olympics was the catalyst for a massive overhaul of Beijing's hotel accommodation; as new luxury hotels were flung up, existing places revamped themselves for the tourist rush and budget chains extended their options in the capital. Now, Beijing has rooms in all price brackets and there are so many of them that travellers are spoilt for choice.

There's no shortage of luxury options, including chains such as **Sofitel** (www.sofitel.com), **Ritz-Carlton** (www.ritzcarlton.com) and **Peninsula** (www.peninsula.com), but Beijing lacks the historic hotels found in Shanghai and Hong Kong, a result of its never having been colonised (except briefly by the Japanese).

Beijing makes up for that with its delightful courtyard hotels, which are mostly located in traditional *hutong* (alleyway) neighbourhoods and have atmosphere in spades, as well as usually boasting a good level of service. The downside is that their rooms tend to be smaller and less luxurious than the ones in the modern four- and five-star hotels.

Midrange hotels are less impressive. They can be found everywhere, but their decor is generally unremarkable, facilities can be old and amenities limited. Nor will many of their staff speak English, unlike in the luxury hotels. Motel-style chains, though, have mushroomed in Beijing. Their design may be generic without much Chinese flavour, but the service is efficient and rooms are clean and modern. Two ubiquitous chains in Beijing worth trying are **Home Inn** (www.homeinns.com) and **Jinjiang Inn** (www.jinjianginns.com).

Budget hotels are generally shabby and worth avoiding. Hostels, however, have sprung up all over central Beijing, particularly in Dongcheng (Map pp40–1) and Xicheng's Houhai Lake area (Map p87, D2-D3), and

lonely planet Hotels & Hostels

Need a place to stay? Find and book it at lonelyplanet.com. Over 300 properties are listed for Beijing, with 65 of those personally visited, thoroughly reviewed and happily recommended by a Lonely Planet author. From hostels to high-end hotels, we've hunted out the places that will bring you unique and special experiences. Read independent reviews by authors and other travellers, and get practical information including amenities, maps and photos. Then reserve your room simply and securely via Hotels & Hostels – our online booking service. It's all at lonelyplanet.com/hotels.

are a terrific option. The staff usually speak good English, while visitor information and tour services are among the best in the city.

Most travellers base themselves in Dongcheng, Xicheng or north Chaoyang. Dongcheng (p38) has most of Beijing's major sights, and many of the city's popular luxury and courtyard hotels are in this district.

West of Dongcheng, Xicheng (p86) has decent hostels and plenty of midrange accommodation, which will put you near the Houhai Lake area's bars, restaurants and shopping. East of Dongcheng, north Chaoyang (p52) is Beijing's nightlife hub and has some of the best restaurants in town. The district has a full range of accommodation, from hostels to boutique hotels and luxury options.

With so many rooms on offer, most hotels slash their listed rates by as much as 40% to 50% for much of the year. Don't be shy about asking for a discount. The exception to this is during the peak tourist season from June to September and public holidays like the Spring Festival/Chinese New Year (p26). You'll need to book well ahead if you're planning to be in town then – visit lonelyplanet.com/hotels, or CTrip (www.english.ctrip.com).

At check-in, guests are required to fill out a registration form with their visa and passport details. The form is then sent to the local Public Security Bureau.

BEST FOR LUXURY
> Grand Hyatt (www.beijing.grand.hyatt.com)
> Peninsula Beijing (http://beijing.peninsula.com)
> Ritz-Carlton Beijing, Financial St (www.ritzcarlton.com)
> St Regis (www.stregis.com/beijing)

BEST COURTYARD HOTELS
> Haoyuan Hotel (www.haoyuanhotel.com)
> Hotel Cote Cour SL (www.hotelcotecoursl.com)
> Red Capital Residence (www.redcapitalclub.com.cn)

BEST HOSTELS
> City Walls Courtyard (www.beijingcitywalls.com)
> Far East International Youth Hostel (www.fareastyh.com)
> Beijing Downtown Backpackers Accommodation (www.backpackingchina.com)

MOST UNFORGETTABLE ATMOSPHERE
> Aman at Summer Palace (www.amanresorts.com)
> Commune by the Great Wall (www.communebythegreatwall.com)

SNAPSHOTS

ARCHITECTURE

In the 1950s Beijing jumped straight from being a walled city packed with the unique, ancient architecture of the Ming and Qing dynasties to the bleak buildings and vistas of Soviet-inspired socialist-realist design. Now, it's making another leap by throwing up the kind of daring, avant-garde structures that many cities shy away from.

Besides obvious sights like the Forbidden City (p10) or the Temple of Heaven (p18), the best of Beijing's traditional architecture are the courtyard homes that can be found in the city's *hutong* (alleyways). These homes are built on a north–south axis with living quarters wrapped around a small courtyard. All are built in strict accordance with feng shui principles to ensure the *qi* (energy) can freely circulate. There are no outside windows, so when the red courtyard gates are shut, it becomes a private world.

Every Ming and Qing building, no matter how big or small, is built along the same principles, though wealthier people added more courtyards and rooms. You could even describe the Forbidden City as the biggest courtyard house of them all.

There are only a handful of buildings that predate the Ming dynasty in Beijing, and all have been rebuilt many times since. It's the same story with the surviving Ming structures around town, as fire, war and weather have taken their toll over the centuries.

But following the Communist Party's takeover of China in 1949, Beijing underwent immense changes. Socialist-realist architecture was the big thing and architects from the old Soviet Union descended on the city to help their 'socialist brothers' modernise the capital, by fashioning a sombre skyline dominated by Stalin's so-called 'wedding cake', or tiered, buildings.

The vast edifices that line Tiananmen Sq (p12) are the prime example of this style of architecture. The hulking China National Museum opened in 1959 and was built to commemorate the 10th anniversary of the founding of the People's Republic of China. The Great Hall of the People, on the opposite side of the square and also built in 1959, is the most imposing structure left over from this period. Thankfully, the Sino-Soviet split in 1960 put an end to the attempt to turn Beijing into Moscow. For more details on modern architecture, see p20.

BEST SOCIALIST ARCHITECTURE

> Beijing Exhibition Centre
  (Map p87, A3)
> Great Hall of the People (p88)
> China National Museum
  (Map pp40–1, B8)

MOST CONTROVERSIAL NEW BUILDINGS

> CCTV Building (p74)
> National Centre for the Performing
  Arts (p91)

BEST TRADITIONAL ARCHITECTURE

> Huguang Guildhall (p84)
> Prince Gong's Residence (p89)
> Mei Lanfang Former Residence (p89)
> Drum and Bell Towers (p42 and p39)
> Chuandixia Village (p113)

MOST EMBRACED NEW BUILDINGS

> Bird's Nest Stadium (p53)
> Capital Museum (p88)

Above Locals call it 'big shorts'; outsiders marvel at the style and grace of the CCTV building (p74)

DRINKING

It's amazing to contemplate, but 20 years ago there weren't any bars in Beijing, save for a few in hotels for foreigners. Now, though, the city's drinking scene has exploded. Whether you want to sip fancy cocktails in a stylish setting, down pints in a pub or hang out in a grungy student bar, you'll be able to find a place to do just that.

As the number of bars has increased dramatically, so they have spread across Beijing. Once famous as the city's main bar street, Sanlitun Lu (Map pp54–5, D4) is now strung with generic tourist traps to be avoided. Instead, head just south to Nansanlitun Lu (Map pp54–5, D5) for some of the city's coolest lounges, or head off the main drag to the bars in the surrounding streets. South Chaoyang (Map p73) has a number of very smart spots that cater to the CBD crowd.

To the east, Dongcheng has an ever-increasing array of hip *hutong* bars. The area behind the Drum and Bell Towers and Nanluogu Xiang *hutong* are good places to head to. Nanluogu Xiang (Map pp40–1, B3) in particular has become one of Beijing's busiest bar streets and is absolutely jumping on the weekends, with crowds spilling out onto the street.

The nearby Houhai Lake area (Map p87, D2-D3) is swamped with bars, many with lovely lakeside views, that are popular with the locals. Be discerning here and avoid the places with aggressive bar touts trying to pull you in. In the northwest of Beijing, the large student population based in Wudaokou keeps the lively bars on and around Chengfu Lu (Map p99, B3) busy.

Although most Chinese would rather sing karaoke on a Friday night, or share a Y2 beer and some street food, than drop Y60 on a cocktail, rising incomes and the more Westernised attitude of young Chinese means that increasingly you'll find a good mix of locals and expats in bars. Some of them are now opening their own places aimed at the locals, rather than the expats who used to keep Beijing's bars afloat.

The free English-language listings magazines (p153) are the best way to find out what the hot new drinking spots are.

SNAPSHOTS

BEST TO IMPRESS
> Centro (p70)
> LAN (p78)
> Mesh (p63)
> Yin (p51)

BEST TO RELAX
> Bed Bar (p90)
> Drum & Bell (p51)
> La Baie Des Anges (p91)
> Stone Boat Bar (p79)

Above The whole gang will be here any minute – one of the bars on the strip around the Houhai Lakes area (p88)

FOOD

Food is an absolute obsession for the Chinese and eating out is the favourite social activity for Beijingers. With over 60,000 restaurants in the capital, and countless thousands of street food stands, they're spoilt for choice and so will you be. Beijing is a foodies' paradise because, apart from serving up the local cuisine and an ever-increasing number of international ones, the city's restaurants offer food from every corner of the country. You can eat your way across China without ever leaving Beijing.

Although there are many regional differences, Chinese cuisine has four main schools, one for each compass point. Beijing food is classified as 'northern cuisine', which makes heavy use of wheat and millet, with noodles and steamed dumplings (*jiaozi*) popular staples. Peking duck (p21) is the city's most famous dish. Beijingers, though, are equally enthusiastic about hotpot, which has Mongol origins, and the local street food (*Beijing xiaochi* 北京小吃) which involves anything that can be whipped up roadside or skewered on a stick.

Sichuan (western cuisine) is popular all over China for its fiery taste, which comes from extensive use of tongue-searing red chilli and flower pepper. Shanghai, or eastern cuisine, is more delicate and sweet and uses a lot of fish and fresh vegetables. Cantonese (southern cuisine) is the Chinese food many foreigners have experienced in their home countries, because most overseas Chinese restaurants are run by people from Hong Kong and southern China. But it's much more exotic in China. It's also the least spicy of all the cuisines.

Dining Chinese-style is a noisy, chaotic and often messy affair. Beijingers like to eat in big groups and they're at their most relaxed and gregarious when sitting around the dining table. Restaurants aren't judged by their decor or service; the only thing that matters is the food and the company. Most Chinese dishes are meant to be eaten communally, with everyone digging in with their chopsticks, and a selection of cold and hot meat, fish and vegetable dishes is the standard order. Don't worry about dropping food; you won't be the only one doing so.

BEST PEKING DUCK
> Beijing Dadong Roast Duck Restaurant (p49)
> Bianyifang Roast Duck Restaurant (p70)
> Hua Jia Yi Yuan (p50)
> Liqun Roast Duck Restaurant (p71)

BEST FOR ROMANCE
> Café Sambal (p89)
> Dall Courtyard (p49)
> Source (p50)

MOST FUN ATMOSPHERE
> Baguo Buyi (p89)
> Makye Ame (p78)
> Xiao Wang's Family Restaurant (p78)
> Xinjiang Red Rose Restaurant (p60)

BEST INTERNATIONAL
> Hatsune (p77)
> Hutong Pizza (p90)
> Maison Boulud (p50)
> Salt (p60)

Above Roast duck, soon to be sliced and laid out with tiny pancakes, dipping sauce, green onions and cucumber (p21)

PARKS & GARDENS

Many of Beijing's parks are former imperial gardens and were off-limits to ordinary Beijingers until after the founding of the People's Republic of China. In Xicheng district, Jingshan Park (p88) was once part of the Forbidden City. The hill in Jingshan, which is not a natural feature in pancake-flat Beijing, was built to protect the palace from the evil spirits coming from the north.

Jingshan is also where Chongzhen, the last Ming emperor, hung himself from a tree as the invading Manchu forces swarmed over the city walls. Nearby, in Xicheng, Beihai Park (p88) was a royal stomping ground from the Yuan dynasty, when it was the site of Kublai Khan's now-vanished palace. During this period, earth was removed to make its enormous lake and the displaced soil was used to form the small middle island, Jade Islet.

Elsewhere, the majority of the city's parks were created from land formerly used by the emperors to perform annual rites to various gods. Though each of the parks is different, all still have the vast altars where the emperors stood while conducting their rituals. These days, however, locals use them for kite flying and taichi practice.

But Chinese parks and gardens are more than just recreational spaces. Unlike Western parks, they are considered to be landscape art and are meant to perfectly balance the *yin* and *yang*. Each garden must have several elements – the main ones being plants, rock, water and pavilions – in order for it to be harmonious. Consequently, the hardness of the rock (*yang*) should balance out the softness of the water (*yin*), while plants are chosen for their symbolic significance as much as for their aesthetics.

BEST ESCAPES FROM POLLUTION
> Beijing Botanic Gardens (p94)
> Fragrant Hills Park (p96)

BEST FORMER RITUAL GROUNDS
> Ditan Park (p42)
> Ritan Park (p74)
> Temple of Heaven (p69)
> Workers' Cultural Palace (p46)

MOST BEAUTIFUL LANDSCAPES
> Beijing Museum of Red Chamber Culture & Art (p82)
> Summer Palace (see the boxed text, p95)

BEST WALKS
> Beihai Park (p88)
> Houhai (see the boxed text, p88)
> Longtan Park (p68)
> Old Summer Palace park (p101)

Above Landscape art or water garden, feng shui (p138) is a cornerstone of the design

SNAPSHOTS

SHOPPING

Shopping is one of Beijing's pleasures – whether you're looking for souvenirs, haggling over pearls or just soaking up the atmosphere at one of the open-air markets. Prices aren't as cheap as they used to be, but good deals are still possible for items like art, scrolls, silk, jewellery, jade and clothing.

Beijing has a huge amount of stores and specialist shopping districts to choose from. In Xuanwu, Liulichang Xijie and Liulichang Dongjie (Map p81, C2), located in a vibrant *hutong* neighbourhood, have been restored as old-style shopping streets and are lined with dozens of stores specialising in inks, paintings and scrolls. This is where Beijing's professional calligraphers, teachers and students come to buy their paper, brushes and calligraphy books. It's also a good place to get a chop, or seal, made.

Nearby, Dazhalan Jie (Map p81, D2-D3) has been a shopping zone for centuries and is home to some of Beijing's oldest stores. Like Liulichang, it's pedestrian only and the bustling *hutong* running off it still retain a medieval flavour.

In Dongcheng, Wangfujing Dajie (Map pp40–1, C5-C6) is the most fashionable shopping strip, anchored by the upmarket Oriental Plaza mall and lined with towering department stores. Elsewhere in the district, trendy clothes, accessory and jewellery stores have overrun Gulou Dongdajie (Map pp40–1, B3) and Nanluogu Xiang (Map pp40–1, B3).

Next door in Chaoyang, clothing from the Silk Market or Yashow Clothing Market is many travellers' favourite buy. There are plenty of malls here too, while further south is the fantastic Panjiayuan Antique Market (p22).

The Houhai Lake area (Map p87, D2-D3) in Xicheng has jewellery and souvenir options, both lakeside and on nearby Yandai Xiejie. Xidan Beidajie (北大街; Map p87, C4-C5), just north of the Xidan subway stop, is where young Beijingers shop for clothes. Mobbed at weekends, it's packed with above- and below-ground malls and department stores.

While handicrafts and kites, traditional paper cuttings and silk scarves all make excellent souvenirs, be wary of buying items the vendor claims are antiques. Not only is it illegal for foreigners to take anything made before 1795 out of the country, but Beijing has mostly been swept of its genuine treasures. What wasn't destroyed or stolen in the wars before 1949 disappeared in the Cultural Revolution or has been smuggled out of the country more recently.

It's the same story for art: almost 100% of all works from China's great 20th-century masters are completely catalogued in private collections and museums. There are, though, plenty of options for buying contemporary art at the galleries in the 798 Art District (p16), even if the work doesn't come cheap.

Prices are generally fixed in malls and department stores, although a 10% discount is sometimes possible if you ask. Markets and antique shops are another matter. Haggle hard – all sellers think foreigners are loaded and in places like Panjiayuan will sometimes ask for 10 times the real price – but remember to keep it friendly. The point of bargaining is not to screw the vendor into the ground, but to find a mutually acceptable transaction. Often, just walking away results in a lower price.

With Beijingers shopping and spending more and more, closing time is fading further into the night. Most malls, markets and shops are open every day, from 9am or 10am and some stay open until 10pm.

In many department stores and older shops, paying for your purchase involves handing over what you want to the salesperson, who gives you a ticket for the cashier, who collects your money and gives you a stamped receipt to take back to the salesperson to exchange for your purchase.

Most up-scale malls and some shops will take international credit cards; others accept only Chinese credit cards. Markets are cash only, so come prepared.

BEST WINDOW SHOPPING
> Dazhalan Jie (Map p81, D2-D3)
> Liulichang Xijie and Liulichang Dongjie (Map p81, C2)
> Nanluogu Xiang (Map pp40–1, B3)
> Wangfujing Dajie (Map pp40–1, C5-C6)

MOST FUN FOR HAGGLING
> Beijing Curio City (p74)
> Panjiayuan Antique Market (p76)
> Pearl Market (p70)
> Sanlitun Yashow Clothing Market (p53)
> Silk Market (p76)

BEST CHINESE FASHION
> Five Colours Earth (p74)
> Lu Ping Trendsetters (p47)

BEST SOUVENIRS
> Bannerman Tang's Toys & Crafts (p46)
> Grifted (p47)
> Plastered T-Shirts (p47)
> Shard Box Store (p76)
> Xing Mu's Handicrafts (p89)
> Zhaoyuange (p48)

ACROBATICS

Chinese acrobatic shows are always a thrill and Beijing's troupes are some of the best in the country. There's nothing quite like seeing young contortionists turn themselves inside out and upside down, while spinning plates on the ends of long sticks, or balancing on poles.

Circus acts have a 2000-year history in China. As far back as the Warring States Period (roughly 475–221 BC) there are mentions of such off-beat activities as dagger juggling and stilt walking. Wuqiao County in Hebei province, which borders Beijing, is believed to have been the original stronghold of Chinese acrobatics.

Routines were developed using simple, everyday objects like sticks, hoops, chairs and jars. Difficult acts to follow include 'Peacock Displaying its Feathers' (a dozen or more people balanced on one bicycle) and 'Pagoda of Bowls' (a performer does everything with her torso except tie it in knots, while balancing a stack of bowls on her foot, head, or both).

Despite these superhuman feats, acrobats, like Peking opera performers, occupied a lowly place in Chinese society. That all changed in the 20th century, however, especially once Chinese troupes (particularly from Beijing) started performing abroad to international acclaim.

Now, professional Chinese acrobats undergo the same rigorous training as future sports stars. Gifted children as young as five or six are singled out and enrolled in schools run by the various acrobatic companies. And, like sport, it is a short career. The typical acrobat retires from performing sometime in their 30s, or whenever their bodies can't take the strain any more.

Chinese acrobats are famous throughout the world for their dazzling feats

CYCLING

Getting around Beijing by bike is one of the most enjoyable ways to experience the city. Yes, there are some mad drivers on the roads, but there are also bike lanes, and Beijing's flat layout makes it ideal for cycling. Above all, you won't be short of company: millions of Beijingers cycle every day.

Dongcheng district is the best area to cycle around. Peddling through the *hutong* around the Drum and Bell Towers, Nanluogu Xiang (Map pp40–1, B3) and the Houhai Lake area (Map p87, D2-D3) is far more fun than sitting in a traffic jam.

Rentals are everywhere, but your safest bet is at your accommodation. If that's not possible, try any *hutong* near a youth hostel or courtyard hotel. Prices are around Y20 to Y30 per day, although the deposit will be Y300 or more. Never leave your passport as surety and make sure to check out the bike, especially the brakes, before you leave.

Don't expect drivers to indicate when on the road. Remember, it's always the cyclist's job to get out of the car's way and not the other way around.

Bike theft is a problem in Beijing, so always park your bike in the city's cycling parks (price 2 mao), where an attendant can watch it.

Cycling is a great way to get around and you won't be the only one on the road

SNAPSHOTS

GALLERIES

The rise of Chinese contemporary art is one of the more extraordinary side effects of China's economic boom. Beijing is now mentioned in the same breath as London, New York and Berlin when it comes to the world's most vibrant artistic communities. It's all the more amazing when you consider that Beijing didn't even have a contemporary art gallery until 1991.

Now, the galleries of the 798 Art District (see picture below and the boxed text, p56) are some of the most-visited places in the city. Their popularity, though, means that some of them have become more commercial, while high rents have driven other galleries out of the area. Nevertheless, 798 is still an essential stop for anyone interested in contemporary art, especially if you have a hankering for experimental art and media installations.

But the art scene is now so firmly entrenched in Beijing that new areas are opening up as artists' colonies. In particular, the Caochangdi neighbourhood, 2km or so north of 798, has seen an influx of galleries and artists in search of cheap studio spaces and is well worth checking out.

If you want to stick closer to town, a handful of established galleries in central Beijing continue to thrive. The Red Gate Gallery (p68) is the best.

BEST FOR FINDING THE NEXT STAR
> Caochangdi
> C5ART (p53)

BEST FOR ESTABLISHED ARTISTS
> Amelie Gallery (see boxed text, p56)
> Galleria Continua (see boxed text, p56)
> Red Gate Gallery (p68)

GAY & LESBIAN

Although there is more domestic media coverage of homosexual issues than ever before in China, most of Beijing's gays and lesbians fly well under the radar. Homosexuality remains a taboo subject within Chinese society generally and few people are willing to come out. That unease is reflected in the low-key nature of the Beijing gay and lesbian scene.

The long-standing Destination (p64), Beijing's only gay club, apart, there are few identifiable gay and lesbian nightlife spots in the city. Homosexuality was classified as a mental disorder in China until as recently as 2001, so not many places are keen to attract the attention of the authorities by advertising themselves as gay and lesbian venues. But some bars, like Mesh (p63) and Yin (p51) are gay friendly on certain nights.

Newcomers to the city can check www.gayographic.cn, which has details of events and parties for the foreign gay and lesbian community in Beijing.

MARTIAL ARTS

Martial arts are as much a part of the Beijing landscape as *hutong,* temples and bicycles. Legions of Beijingers, especially the older generation, begin the day by stretching a leg in the city parks or their apartment compounds.

Three main martial arts and exercises are popular in China: *taijiquan* (taichi), which is known for its slow, fluid movements; *gongfu* (kung fu), famous for its focus on self-defence; and *qigong,* associated with traditional Chinese medicine and focused on mental and physical well-being.

Taichi is the most popular. The yang style, with its uniform pacing, is the style most Beijingers practise. But walk around town and you'll also see lots of wu-style practitioners, with their smaller and more pronounced stances and motions. Chen-style taichi is the easiest to recognise and the most fun to watch, as practitioners perform super-slow movements before exploding into quick, powerful movements.

The **Jinghua Wushu Association** (京华武术协会; Map pp54-5, E2; ☎ 135 2228 3751; basement, Kempinski Hotel, Liangmaqiao Lu 亮马桥凯宾斯基饭店底层; ⊙ Liangmaqiao) has English-language instructors. The China Culture Center (p149) also offers occasional one-off classes that include anything from beginners' taichi to *taijijian* (taichi with swords) at the Altar of the Earth at Ditan Park (p42).

The best place to watch people practising their moves is the Temple of Heaven Park (p69), where crowds of taichi devotees gather to sway and lunge as the sun rises. With a turnout regularly in the hundreds, it's a sight worth waking up for. If you're not a morning person, you can check out some death-defying martial-arts moves at the Red Theatre's spectacular show *The Legend of Kung Fu* (see p71).

Youngsters practising their martial arts moves

MUSEUMS

Beijing's museums have made great strides in the last few years. Once characterised by chinglish captions, or none at all, sullen staff and a deadening, lifeless atmosphere, there are now a few, like the outstanding Capital Museum (p88), which can rank with the best in London and New York.

Nor is there any shortage of museums to visit in Beijing. There are institutions devoted to everything from architecture to sandalwood and it would take weeks to get round them all. Most of the interesting ones are in and around Dongcheng district in central Beijing. Many are in historic buildings, and don't forget that the Forbidden City is, amongst other things, a complex of mini-museums with rotating exhibitions.

Xicheng has its share of museums worth visiting too. Around the Houhai Lake (Map p87, C2-D2) the old courtyard homes of some of Beijing's most illustrious writers and artists have been turned into shrines to them. Many lack enough English captions or context to be meaningful to foreigners, but the Mei Lanfang Former Residence (p89) is a notable exception. In Haidian, the Military Museum (p96) keeps young boys, and older ones too, out of trouble by letting them crawl over tanks.

MOST STUNNING EXHIBITS
> Capital Museum (p88)
> Poly Art Museum (p46)

BEST FOR IMPERIAL HISTORY
> Beijing Imperial City Art Museum (p39)
> Forbidden City (see the boxed text, p44)
> Summer Palace's Wenchang Gallery (see the boxed text, p95)

BEST FOR ART
> National Art Museum of China (p42)
> Beijing World Art Museum (p94)

QUIRKIEST COLLECTIONS
> Beijing Police Museum (p39)
> Forbidden City's Clocks and Watches Gallery (see the boxed text, p44)
> Great Bell Temple (p100)
> Military Museum (p96)

TEMPLES

Temples are scattered throughout every district in Beijing. But getting 'templed out' is unlikely. All Beijing's temples are unique in their own way and it's worth taking the time to visit several. By stepping through their gates, you leave the hustle of modern Beijing behind and enter a timeless world of solemn worshippers, busy monks and plumes of incense smoke wafting through the air.

Every school of Chinese thought, Buddhist, Confucian and Taoist, is represented in Beijing. But whatever philosophy they adhere to, Chinese temples are laid out in the same way as traditional courtyard homes (see also p118): along a north–south axis according to the principles of feng shui. The middle courtyard area contains the prayer halls, while the surrounding quarters usually house the resident monks.

Chongwen's colossal Temple of Heaven (p18) is the best known, while Dongcheng's Lama Temple (p42) attracts the most worshippers. Nearby is the Confucius Temple (p42), the country's second-largest shrine to the famous philosopher.

The differences between Buddhist and Taoist temples aren't always immediately apparent, but the monks have distinctive appearances. Buddhist monks usually have shaved heads, while Taoists have their long hair tied into a topknot.

Beijing's temples welcome visitors, but always ask permission first if you want to take photos of the monks or worshippers.

MOST MORBID
> Dongyue Temple (p53)

MOST HISTORIC
> Fayuan Temple (p82)
> Miaoying Temple White Dagoba (p89)
> Temple of Heaven (p69)

MOST SERENE
> Confucius Temple (p42)
> Zhihua Temple (p74)

BEST TIBETAN
> Lama Temple (p42)
> Wuta Temple (p96)

A sculpted column stands before Tiananmen Gate (p46)

BACKGROUND

HISTORY

Located on a plain, prone to dust storms, lacking a river and nowhere near the sea, Beijing is hardly the ideal place to establish a capital city. By AD 938, though, it was an auxiliary centre for the ruling Liao dynasty, who called it Yanjing, which is still the name of Beijing's local beer. Subsequently sacked and destroyed by Genghis Khan in 1215, Beijing was the Mongol capital of China for a century or so. It wasn't until the Ming dynasty that it became a truly Chinese city.

The credit for that goes to Yongle (1360–1424), the third Ming emperor. Much of what you see in today's Beijing, including the Forbidden City and the Temple of Heaven, is down to him. The Ming rulers got busy outside town too, reinforcing the Great Wall and manning it with a million soldiers. That, though, cut no ice with the Manchus, who swept down from the northeast, overthrew the Ming and established the Qing dynasty (1644–1911).

Under the Qing, the Han Chinese were forced to live in the south of Beijing outside the city walls, in what are the present-day districts of Chongwen (p66) and Xuanwu (p80). At the same time, the Qing did much to improve Beijing, building summer palaces, pagodas and temples. They also adopted Chinese culture as their own, boosting Peking opera, calligraphy and painting.

But the last years of the Qing dynasty were some of the most challenging Beijing had ever known, as the city bore the brunt of the Second Opium War (1856–60), the Taiping Rebellion (1851–64) and the Boxer Rebellion (1900).

THE COMMUNIST REVOLUTION

When Empress Cixi died in 1908, she bequeathed power to two-year-old Puyi (Aisin Gioro Puyi), China's last emperor. But the Qing dynasty, battered by years of war and internal power struggles and with little control outside Beijing, was about to collapse. The revolution of 1911 paved the way for the Kuomintang (or Nationalists) to take power, and the Republic of China was declared, with Sun Yat-sen as president. That made precious little difference to China's parlous state, as warlords continued to carve up huge swaths of the country, while the foreign powers controlled important economic zones in major ports like Shanghai and Tianjin.

Crippling poverty and splintered rule were a recipe for further rebellion. Beijing's students were at the forefront of protests and it was at Peking University that a young librarian named Mao Zedong (1893–1976) began reading the works of Karl Marx. The Chinese Communist Party emerged and joined with the Kuomintang to wrestle power from the northern warlords. A year later (1927), the Kuomintang turned on the communists, who fled into China's vast interior. The Chinese civil war was under way.

The Japanese takeover of Beijing in 1937 saw the Kuomintang fleeing the city too and resulted in an uneasy eight-year truce with the communists. But after Japan's defeat in 1945, hostilities resumed and this time there would only be one winner. In 1949 the communists marched into Beijing and Mao proclaimed the People's Republic of China, while the Kuomintang fled to Taiwan, along with China's gold reserves and many of the Forbidden City's treasures.

AFTERMATH

Beijing underwent huge changes in the first decade of communist rule. The mighty city walls were pulled down, and hundreds of temples and historic buildings were demolished. The turmoil continued in the 1960s, when Mao launched the Cultural Revolution. Though this wasn't the most costly of Mao's mistakes in terms of lives lost, the period between 1966 and his death in 1976 was still catastrophic for China.

Chaos ruled, as Mao incited the masses to rid China of the bourgeois elements he claimed were holding back the revolution. Red Guards, Mao's youth army, roamed the streets, the education system collapsed, neighbours informed on neighbours and families were split, as hysteria about 'capitalist-roadsters' saw millions persecuted.

A great deal of damage was done to Beijing's ancient temples and other historic buildings, the scars of which can still be seen today. It's ironic that the HQ of the Cultural Revolution in Beijing was at a site now occupied by a swish shopping plaza that houses the popular nightclub GT Banana (p79).

After Mao's death, Deng Xiaoping, his one-time protégé, launched the economic reforms that have led to China's emergence as a global superpower. The country began to open up and Westerners started to visit. Temples and monuments were restored, while in Beijing thousands of ancient *hutong* (alleyways) were bulldozed to make way for skyscrapers and apartment blocks.

China's leaders had embraced capitalism, but they had no intention of changing politically. In 1989, the pro-democracy student demonstrations in Tiananmen Sq ended in hundreds of protestors dying at the hands of the army. Today, political dissent has been consigned to a subterranean level, with those who publicly oppose the Communist Party harassed or arrested.

Staging the hugely successful 2008 Olympics was the cue for Beijing to be transformed again. Infrastructure has been vastly improved, new buildings have changed the skyline and Beijing is now a true world city. Nevertheless, the conflict between economic freedom and the absolute power wielded by the Communist Party presents huge challenges for the future. After all, many a dynasty has risen and fallen in Beijing.

LIFE AS A BEIJINGER

It's no exaggeration to say that Beijingers have never had it so good. For young people especially, the combination of rising incomes and greater access to education means they are experiencing a freedom that was unknown to their parents. They have become enthusiastic consumers and are far more independent, marrying later, as well as divorcing more frequently than before.

The goal of a better life is everybody's dream. Owning an apartment and a car is what people aim for, and increasing numbers of them are choosing to set up their own businesses to achieve that. The days when people looked to the state to provide jobs and security are long gone.

But despite all the changes, the family remains the very core of Chinese society. Often, three generations live together under the same roof. China's One-Child Policy, introduced in 1979 to curb population growth, has created the so-called '4-2-1' phenomenon, where families consist of four grandparents, two parents and one child.

FENG SHUI

Literally meaning 'wind and water', feng shui is a collection of ancient geomantic principles that sees bodies of water and landforms directing the cosmic currents of the universal *qi* (energy). Feng shui guidelines create a positive path for *qi*, which can maximise a person's wealth, happiness, longevity and fertility. Ignoring the principles and blocking the flow can spell disaster. Temples, tombs, houses and even whole cities have been built in feng shui fashion to harmonise with the surrounding landscape. Within a building, the order of rooms and arrangement of furniture can also inhibit or enhance *qi* flow.

Now, the older generation rely on the young for subsistence and care, and in return perform much of the child care. It is the elderly, too, who maintain the traditional lifestyle of Beijingers, hanging out in the *hutong* and streets chatting and playing mah jong, or roaming the city parks. Their children are more likely to be watching the latest soap opera on TV.

Confucianism, Taoism and Buddhism are the dominant beliefs in Beijing. Buddhism and Taoism give reverence to gods and goddesses who preside over earth and the afterlife. Confucianism is more of a philosophy that defines codes of conduct and a patriarchal pattern of obedience; respect flows upwards from child to adult, woman to man and subject to ruler. Not surprisingly, it was adopted by the state for two millennia and is still quoted approvingly by the current government.

ARTS
MUSIC

Many Chinese folk songs can be traced back several hundred years and traditional musical concerts are still popular in Beijing. Performances feature the *sheng* (reed flute), the *erhu* (two-stringed fiddle), the *huqin* (two-stringed viola), the moon-shaped *yueqin* (four-stringed guitar), the *guzheng* (zither), the *pipa* (lute) and the ceremonial *suon* (trumpet). These instruments are also the accompaniment to Peking opera.

Beijing, though, is also the capital of China's contemporary music scene. Rock bands started emerging in the late 1980s. Now, you can find everything from indie, punk and metal bands, to jazz, hip-hop and techno DJs in the capital. The current darlings of the indie scene are Carsick Cars. Also popular are PK14 and Lonely China Day. Mickey Zhang is the top local DJ and is a ubiquitous presence at Beijing dance parties.

PAINTING

A traditional Chinese painting is very different from a Western picture. The brush line, which varies in thickness and tone, is the important feature; shading is regarded as a foreign technique; and colour plays only a minor symbolic and decorative role. Figure painting dominated the scene from the Han dynasty (206 BC–AD 220), until Taoist painters began landscape painting in the 4th and 5th centuries.

It wasn't until the 20th century that there was any real departure from tradition. In the early days of communism, artistic talent was employed to glorify the revolution in propaganda paintings. In the last decade, though, one of the most important art scenes in the world has grown up in Beijing. China's top artists include Ai Weiwei, Yue Minjun and Cai Guoqiang. For more on the contemporary art scene, see p16.

FILMS

Although Shanghai was where the Chinese film industry began, Beijing has been the movie capital of China since 1949. The vast majority of Chinese film-makers and actors graduate from the Beijing Film Academy and the Central Drama Academy in Nanluogu Xiang (Map pp40–1, B3).

Films are still subject to strict scrutiny by the censors, and two of the best recent movies set in Beijing were both banned. 2007's *Lost in Beijing*, directed by Li Yu, captures the feeling of a city in flux and the effect that has on its inhabitants. Lou Ye's *Summer Palace* (2006) relates the story of the obsessive love affair between two Peking University students and is set against the backdrop of the Tiananmen Sq demonstrations.

Zhang Yuan's films veer between quirky romances like 2003's *Green Tea* and the controversial *East Palace, West Palace* (1996) with its taboo look at gay life in the capital. The finest recent comedies are those of Feng Xiaogang. His 2003 movie *Cell Phone* skilfully satirises the emerging Beijing middle classes and was a huge hit in China.

For films about old Beijing, look no further than Bernardo Bertolucci's *The Last Emperor* (1987), which won a truckload of Oscars and chronicles the demise of the Qing dynasty. Equally good is Beijinger Chen Kaige's beautifully shot *Farewell My Concubine* (1993), set in the world of Peking opera before and after WWII.

FURTHER READING

Beijing has produced some of China's most famous and respected authors. Lao She is a giant of 20th-century Chinese literature, best known for his 1936 novel *Rickshaw Boy*, about the grim life of a Beijing rickshaw driver in the 1920s, and the play *Teahouse*. Lu Xun started his writing career while teaching at Peking University after WWI and his short stories have seen him acclaimed as the father of modern Chinese literature. Other important early 20th-century writers who lived in Beijing include the novelist Mao Dun and poet Guo Moruo.

When the communists came to power, writing became a hazardous occupation and many writers retired or were persecuted. Nowadays, the situation has improved, although books are still banned if the censors don't like them. Most young Chinese authors start their writing careers on the internet, where they have more freedom to express themselves.

The undoubted star of modern Chinese literature is Wang Shuo, who grew up on a military base in Beijing and writes violently satirical novels that use a lot of Beijing slang. Some, like *Please Don't Call Me Human,* have been translated into English, while others have been adapted into successful films.

Another contemporary novelist who uses Beijing as a backdrop is Ma Jian. His 2008 novel *Beijing Coma* looks back at the 1989 Tiananmen protests from the perspective of a participant who has been left in a coma by the violent end to the demonstrations. Beijinger Annie Wang's *The People's Republic of Desire* is a trenchant, often amusing account of the lives of Beijing's middle-class women.

Non-fiction books about Beijing worth checking out include *Twilight in the Forbidden City* (1934) by Reginald F Johnston, which describes his experiences tutoring Puyi, China's last emperor. *The Siege at Peking* (1959) is an excellent account of the Boxer Rebellion by Peter Fleming. More recently, Rachel DeWoskin's *Foreign Babes in Beijing: Behind the Scenes of a New China* (2005) is a fun memoir of the author's time starring in a Chinese soap opera, just as the capital was receiving an influx of foreigners. *Beijing: From Imperial Capital to Olympic City* (2007), by Lillian M Li, Alison Dray-Novey and Haili Kong, offers a solid, comprehensive overview of Beijing's history.

GOVERNMENT & POLITICS

The Chinese Communist Party (CCP) has maintained its grip on power ever since 1949. Opposition is not tolerated and CCP officials, sometimes called cadres, run China at every level from the national government to the smallest village.

STRINGS ATTACHED

Guanxi, or 'connections', is hugely important in China; you're either in the loop or you're not. Having *guanxi* is especially crucial in business life – there's a thin line between *guanxi* and corruption – but it applies in almost all areas of society. Need a ticket for a sold-out train? Or want first dibs on an apartment in that hot new complex? *Guanxi* can be the answer. Getting *guanxi* is no easy task; for most people it comes via family and your college. But if you can offer access to something not easily attainable, then you'll make friends quickly in China.

An opaque organisation with around 70 million members, the CCP is led by Hu Jintao (b 1942), China's current president and also the head of the armed forces. Now in his second five-year term, Hu has continued to push forward China's economic development, while cracking down on any sign of dissent. The Chinese Premier is Wen Jiabao (b 1942), perhaps the most popular politician in China.

Like other sizeable cities, Beijing is an independent municipality with its own government, although it answers to the central government. As the capital, Beijing is home to all the major national and political institutions.

ECONOMY

China is the third-largest economy in the world (after the United States and Japan) and is expected to overtake Japan in the next couple of years. With annual economic growth hovering around 8%, China is likely to be the world's biggest economy in our lifetime.

Nevertheless, China faces enormous and unique problems. There is a rising and extreme gap between the rich and the poor, with the 700 million people who live in the countryside still mired in poverty. Corruption remains a thorn in the side of the economy, and is a source of huge anger among ordinary citizens. And the high cost of health care and education means people are reluctant to spend heavily on consumer items. As a consequence, the economy continues to be driven by cheap exports and massive public-spending projects.

As the capital and home of many of the country's wealthiest people, Beijing is something of an exception to the rest of China. But despite all the shiny shops and flash cars, many Beijingers, especially those over 50 and the army of migrant workers in the city, have missed out on the economic boom. Unemployment is rising too, while spiralling property prices have made buying an apartment much harder for ordinary people.

ENVIRONMENT

Once infamous for its appalling air pollution, Beijing is a much cleaner city than it was. Polluting industries have been shut down, or shunted off elsewhere, and the air quality is much improved. Nevertheless, there are still days when the smog obscures buildings and the air-pollution index is far higher than the levels recommended by the World Health Organization.

The main cause of the pollution is the 3.5 million cars in the city. With 1000 to 1500 new vehicles taking to Beijing's roads every day, the local government operates a scheme based on odd and even license-plate numbers that keeps cars off the roads for one day of the week. It is hoped that, as new subway lines continue to open, more people can be persuaded to use public transport instead of their cars.

Apart from air pollution, Beijing's biggest environmental concern is its lack of water. So parched is Beijing that rain-inducing chemicals are regularly fired into the clouds. Long dependant on siphoning off water from nearby provinces, the capital is pinning its hopes on the massive South-North Water Transfer Project, which is designed to divert water from the far-off Yangtze River to Beijing. Though the project was meant to be completed by 2010, the water is now projected to start flowing in 2014. If it doesn't work, Beijingers face the very real prospect of water rationing in the near future.

DIRECTORY
TRANSPORT
ARRIVAL & DEPARTURE

International travellers arrive and depart from Beijing's Capital International Airport. Travellers going to or coming from Hong Kong and Shanghai have rail and air options.

AIR

Beijing's **Capital International Airport** (北京首都国际机场; http://en.bcia.com.cn) is about 25km northeast of the city centre. International arrivals and departures use both Terminal 2 and the new Terminal 3. All Air China flights use Terminal 3. Shuttles link the terminals. The Airport Express, a light-rail link, runs between Terminals 2 and 3 and Sanyuanqiao station on line 10 of the subway network and Dongzhimen station on lines 2 and 13.

Departure taxes are included in plane ticket prices. For info on taxis from the airport, see the boxed text, p148.

TRAIN

A daily train service runs to and from Hong Kong (Y556 hard sleeper, 26 hours) leaving and arriving from **Beijing West Railway Station** (北京西站; ☎ 5182 6273). Several fast ('Z') trains run daily to and from Shanghai (Y478 to Y499, 11½ hours) leaving and arriving from the main **Beijing Railway Station** (北京站). Unless you speak some Chinese, buying tickets at the stations can be an overwhelming and chaotic experience. Most travellers prefer to pay a small surcharge and book them through their accommodation. Tickets can also be bought online at www.chinatripadvisor.com and www.china-train-ticket.com if you're in China.

VISA

Visas are required for everyone visiting mainland China. A standard

CLIMATE CHANGE & TRAVEL

Travel – especially air travel – is a significant contributor to global climate change. At Lonely Planet, we believe that all who travel have a responsibility to limit their personal impact. As a result, we have teamed with Rough Guides and other concerned industry partners to support Climate Care, which allows people to offset the greenhouse gases they are responsible for with contributions to energy-saving projects and other climate-friendly initiatives in the developing world. Lonely Planet offsets all staff and author travel.

For more information, turn to the responsible-travel pages on www.lonelyplanet.com. For details about offsetting your carbon emissions and a carbon calculator, go to www.climatecare.org.

Getting To & From Terminals 2 & 3

	Taxi	Airport bus	Subway
Pick-up point	outside Exit 5 at arrivals/ 1st floor Terminal 3	outside Exit 11 at arrivals/ 1st floor Terminal 3	follow signs in terminals
Drop-off points	anywhere	line 3: Dongzhimen, Beijing Railway Station; line 4: Youyi Hotel (Renmin University of China), Beijing TV Station; line 2: Yuyang Hotel, Chaoyangmen, Dongdaqiao	last stop Dongzhimen subway station
Duration	to Tiananmen Sq 60min (light traffic)	average 60-90min to last stop (light traffic)	25min
Cost	to Tiananmen Sq Y90-100 (light traffic)	Y16	Y30
Other	Y15 airport expressway toll	line 3 runs 6.30am-10.30pm to airport, 6.30am-11pm from airport; line 2 runs 7.30am-last flight; line 4 runs 7am-11pm	
Contact	flag down on street	http://en.bcia.com.cn /harbor-guide	www.bjsubway.com/ens /iarrive.shtml/index.html

30-day, single-entry visa is readily available from Chinese embassies and consulates and usually takes three to five working days.

GETTING AROUND

Beijing is a vast, sprawling city, which makes getting around a time-consuming process. Heavy traffic can slow buses and taxis to a near standstill during rush hour. The subway is the quickest way to get around at those times, and with all the new lines that have opened you can get most places on it. Taxis are cheap and plentiful,

except when it rains, but are best avoided between 8am and 10am and 5pm and 7pm, when travel times can double or triple.

BICYCLE

For information on cycling around Beijing, see p129.

BOAT

Boats (Y45/75 one way/return) travel from Xicheng district to the Summer Palace (see the boxed text, p95) along Beijing's Qing-era canal network. They run hourly from 10am to 4pm May to

Recommended Modes of Transport

	Lama Temple	Sanlitun Lu	Panjiayuan Antique Market
Lama Temple	n/a	taxi 20min	subway to Jingsong 45min
Sanlitun Lu	taxi 20min	n/a	subway to Jingsong 15min
Panjiayuan Antique Market	subway to Yonghegong-Lama Temple 45min	subway to Nongzhanguan 10min	n/a
Temple of Heaven	subway to Yonghegong-Lama Temple 20min	subway to Nongzhanguan 40min	taxi 15min
Niujie Mosque	subway to Yonghegong-Lama Temple 40min	subway to Nongzhanguan 45min	subway to Jingsong 40min
Houhai Lake	taxi & subway to Yonghegong-Lama Temple 10min	taxi 25min	taxi & subway to Jingsong 50min
Summer Palace	subway to Yonghegong-Lama Temple 45min	subway to Nongzhanguan 50min	subway to Jingsong 1hr

October. You can catch them at the dock behind the zoo (Map p93, C4), or the dock behind the nearby Beijing Exhibition Centre (Map p87, A3).

BUS

Overcrowded and frustratingly slow, Beijing's city buses aren't very practical for those on short visits and are problematic for non-Chinese speakers. However, two bus stations offer direct services to some far-flung sights. The buses take you to and from the destinations, but there's no guided tour; you explore on your own.

The **Beijing Sightseeing Bus Station** (☎ 24hr info line 8353 1111), on the west side of Tiananmen Sq, is the handiest to use. Buses to Badaling Great Wall (Y100, see p108) leave when full between 7.30am and 11.30am. Count on a six-hour trip; you'll have around two hours at the wall itself. Another option here is the bus that takes in both Badaling and the Ming Tombs (Y160; see p110). Buses leave between 6.30am and 10.30am; it's a full-day trip.

There's another tour bus station near the South Cathedral on Qianmen Xidajie (Map p81,

Temple of Heaven	Niujie Mosque	Houhai Lake	Summer Palace
subway to Tiantandongmen 20min	subway to Caishikou 40min	subway to Gulou Dajie 10min & taxi	subway to Yiheyuan 45min
subway to Tiantandongmen 40min	subway to Caishikou 45min	taxi 25 min	subway to Yiheyuan 50min
taxi 15min	subway to Caishikou 40min	subway to Gulou Dajie 50min & taxi	subway to Yiheyuan 1hr
n/a	subway to Caishikou 30min	subway to Gulou Dajie 30min & taxi	subway to Yiheyuan 1hr
subway to Tiantandongmen 30min	n/a	subway to Gulou Dajie 35min & taxi	subway to Yiheyuan 40min
taxi & subway to Tiantandongmen 30min	taxi & subway to Caishikou 35min	n/a	taxi & subway to Yiheyuan 35min
subway to Tiantandongmen 1hr	subway to Caishikou 40min	subway to Gulou Dajie 35min & taxi	n/a

D2). It's less user-friendly, but it does have a weekend bus (12) to Simatai Great Wall (p109). The buses leave at 8.30am and cost Y60; you get around four hours at the wall.

SUBWAY

Beijing's subways start running between 5am and 6am and close between 10.30pm and 11pm, depending on the line. Buy your ticket (Y2) inside the stations. Trains run every few minutes. In this book, the nearest subway station is noted after the subway icon (🚇) in each listing.

TAXI

The flag fall and first 3km is Y10. After that, it's Y2 for each kilometre. Between 11pm and 6am a 20% surcharge is added to the flag-fall metered fare. Taxi drivers are generally very honest, but they do not speak English, so have your destination written down in characters, or circled on a Chinese-language map. At the end of the trip, pay what's on the meter plus any expressway tolls the driver has paid. Once your ride is under way, the driver should turn on the meter. If he or she doesn't, ask them to turn it on (da biao 打表).

TAXIS FROM THE AIRPORT

A long-running and well-established illegal taxi ring operates inside the arrivals hall of Terminal 2. One man acts as a tout for drivers outside and lures exhausted travellers to fake cabs that charge Y300 (or more) for rides into town. Don't fall for this – make sure you line up at the official taxi stand outside. There are far fewer touts at Terminal 3.

The majority of Beijing taxi drivers are honest, but travellers have occasionally reported problems on the run from the airport into town. Usually, this involves the driver not turning on the meter and charging over the odds. Airport authorities have now started cracking down. The staff at the airport taxi stand write down the taxi number and your destination on a 'passenger direct card', so you can follow up if you think you've been overcharged.

Ask for the receipt (*fapiao;* 发票) when your trip is over. The driver's number will be on it, so you'll be able to track them down if you've left something in the car or need to make a complaint. It's possible to hire taxis for the day, but you must negotiate the rate with the driver depending on where you want to go; expect to pay Y400 minimum.

PRACTICALITIES
BUSINESS HOURS

Offices, banks and government departments are generally open Monday to Friday from 9am to 5pm or 6pm. Shops, malls and department stores are normally open from 10am to 9pm or 10pm. Restaurants are open from 11am to 10pm or 11pm, although some will shut between 2pm and 5pm. Most sights are open daily, including public holidays, although some will close on Monday.

DISCOUNTS

Children under a certain height (normally 1.2m) often get in free or half price at sights. If you can produce a student card or an ISIC card (www.isiccard.com) you may get a discount, although some sights only offer them to people studying at Chinese universities. For details about the useful Beijing Museum Pass, see the boxed text, p46.

ELECTRICITY

Electricity is 220V, 50 Hz. Beijing plugs vary, so you'll see up to four different sorts around town. Bring a good plug-adaptor from home, although they are available to buy in Beijing.

EMERGENCIES

Compared to most cities of its size, Beijing is one of the safest urban centres in the world. Serious or violent crimes against visitors are extremely rare. But be on your guard against pickpockets on public transport, counterfeit money (see the boxed text, p153) and certain scams targeted at foreigners, notably the airport taxi scam (see the boxed text, opposite). See also the boxed text, p48.

HOLIDAYS

New Year's Day 1 January
Spring Festival (Chinese New Year) Generally held in January and February; 14 February 2010, 3 February 2011
International Women's Day 8 March
International Labour Day 1 May
Youth Day 4 May
International Children's Day 1 June
Anniversary of the Founding of the Chinese Communist Party 1 July
Anniversary of the founding of the People's Liberation Army 1 August
National Day 1 October

INFORMATION & ORGANISATIONS

The **China Culture Center** (Map pp54–5, F1; ☎ 6432 9341; www.chinaculturecenter .org; Room 101, Kent Centre, 29, Anjialou, Liangmaqiao Lu) is geared to expats but is open to everyone and offers excellent English-language tours, lectures and courses.

INTERNET

Beijing's internet cafes (*wangba* 网吧) are often squirreled away down *hutong* (alleyways), in basements or on the upper floors of anonymous buildings, so you'll need to keep your eyes peeled for the Chinese characters. They're mostly populated by chain-smoking gamers; expect to pay between Y2 and Y4 an hour. Most of the time, you're required to show ID, so bring your passport. Internet access is readily available at hostels for around Y10 an hour, and in most hotels, where you'll pay anything from Y30 an hour, depending on the class of hotel. Conversely, if you have your own laptop, broadband access in rooms is often free. The government censors routinely block access to certain foreign sites critical of China.

Wi-fi (wireless internet; *gaobaozhen* 高保真) zones are now very common in Beijing. All the cafes listed in this book, and many of the bars and restaurants, have wi-fi.

INTERNET RESOURCES

In addition to www.lonelyplanet .com, interesting sites worth checking are www.thebeijinger .com for the latest news on the bar, club and restaurant scene, www.chinasmack.com for what China's netizens are talking about, and www.danwei.org for insights into Chinese media and urban life. The site www.zhong wen.com offers English-Chinese translations.

DIRECTORY

LANGUAGE

The official language of the People's Republic of China is Putonghua, based on (but not identical to) the Beijing Mandarin dialect.

Written Chinese script is based on ancient pictograph characters that have been simplified over time; while over 56,000 characters have been verified, an educated Chinese person knows and uses between 6000 and 8000 characters. Pinyin has been developed as a Romanisation of Mandarin using English letters, but many Beijingers cannot read it. In this book we've used a simplified version of Pinyin, ie without the tone marks.

A growing number of Beijingers speak some English; in tourist hotels and restaurants and at major sights you'll get along OK without Mandarin. But if you venture into shops, neighbourhoods or conversations that are off the tourist track, you may find yourself lost for words. Names and addresses are provided in Chinese characters throughout this book to use when you're taking taxis. It's also useful to have the concierge of your hotel write down your address in Chinese before you go anywhere.

For a user-friendly guide, with pronunciation tips and a comprehensive phrase list (including script that you can show to people rather than speak), get a copy of Lonely Planet's *Mandarin* phrasebook.

BASICS

Refer also to Lonely Planet's Quick Reference section on the inside front cover of this guidebook.

Hello.
   Ni hao.   你好。
Goodbye.
   Zaijian.   再见。
Please.
   Qing.   请。
Thank you.
   Xiexie.   谢谢。
Yes.
   Shide.   是的。
No. (don't have)
   Mei you.   没有。
No. (not so)
   Bushi.   不是。
Do you speak English?
   Ni hui shuo Yingyu ma?   你会说英语吗？

Do you understand?
   Dong ma?   懂吗？
I understand.
   Wo tingdedong.   我听得懂。

Could you please…?
   Ni neng buneng…?   你能不能…？
   repeat that
   chongfu   重复
   speak more slowly
   shuo man dianr   说慢点儿
   write it down
   xie xialai   写下来

EATING & DRINKING

I don't want MSG.
   Wo bu yao weijing.   我不要味精。
I'm vegetarian.
   Wo chi su.   我吃素。

COUNTERFEIT MONEY

Counterfeit money is common in Beijing, so expect heavy inspection of your paper money before it is accepted. Foreigners are often prime targets for fake bills – especially with 50- and 100-yuan notes. To check the money yourself, turn the bill Mao-side up and stroke the bottom right-hand corner. The design should feel raised. Next, hold it to the light: a ghostly Mao should be hovering on the left-hand side. Don't be shy about handing suspicious money back. Vendors will usually hand you a different bill without a fuss.

Paper notes are issued in denominations of one, five, 10, 20, 50 and 100 yuan and one and five jiao. You may occasionally see a 2-*kuai* or *mao* note, although they are rare now. Coins come in denominations of one yuan, one and five jiao, and one, two and five fen.

TRAVELLERS CHEQUES

Travellers cheques issued by leading banks and issuing agencies like American Express and Visa can be cashed in Beijing at the Bank of China, exchange desks at the airport and up-scale hotels. If you're doing any day trips, cash cheques beforehand, as banks on Beijing's outskirts and in the countryside may not handle travellers cheques.

NEWSPAPERS & MAGAZINES

Beijing has a number of English-language listings magazines, which are a valuable source of information on what's going on each month in terms of events. They also list the addresses in Chinese of many restaurants, bars and clubs, so you can show them to taxi drivers. The best of the bunch are *The Beijinger* (see p149) and *Time Out Beijing* (www.timeout. com.cn/en/beijing).

There are two state-run English-language newspapers: *China Daily*, a broadsheet, *Global Times* a tabloid. Both follow the government line and are not exciting reads.

ORGANISED TOURS

The **China Culture Center** (see p149) offers the best-quality English-language tours in Beijing, covering everything from architecture to the *hutong*. Check its website for the schedule. Otherwise, many hotels and hostels organise tours.

PHOTOGRAPHY & VIDEO

Film and digital photo equipment and accessories are available all over Beijing, often near major tourist sites. There are branches of Kodak Express everywhere; it sells film and memory cards, and you can burn CDs for Y20. Most hostels will burn CDs too.

TELEPHONE

International and domestic calls are easily made from your hotel room or public phones. Local calls from hotel rooms are mostly free (check first), but international calls are expensive and it's better to use a phonecard (see right). Local calls can be made from public phones (usually yellow or orange) at newspaper stands and hole-in-the-wall shops. You pay the owner when you finish.

To call a Beijing number from abroad, dial the international access code (☎ 00 in the UK, 011 in the USA), dial the country code for China (☎ 86) and then the area code for Beijing (☎ 010), dropping the first zero. Then dial the local number. For telephone calls within the same city, drop the area code. If calling internationally from Beijing or from China, drop the first zero of the area or city code after dialling the international access code (☎ 00) and receiving-country code. Then dial the number you wish to call.

CHINESE CITY CODES
Beijing ☎ 010
Hong Kong ☎ 852
Shanghai ☎ 021

COUNTRY CODES
Australia ☎ 61
Canada ☎ 1
France ☎ 33

New Zealand ☎ 64
UK ☎ 44
USA ☎ 1

MOBILE PHONES
Your cell phone from home should work in Beijing (check it's been unlocked for overseas use before leaving). The cheapest way to use a mobile in Beijing is to pick up a local SIM card (Y60 to Y100) from one of the many China Mobile or China Unicom shops. Credit-charging cards (*chongzhi ka* 充值卡; Y50 or Y100) are sold at most convenience stores and newspaper stands. Calls are less than Y1 a minute.

PHONECARDS
IP (internet phone) cards (*IP Ka* IP卡) are best for making international calls and come in various denominations. Most cards either have English-language instructions on them, or an English-language option once you dial the card number. IC (integrated circuit; *IC Ka* IC卡) cards are for domestic calls and can be used at most public phones. IP and IC cards are sold at newspaper stands, small shops, China Telecom offices and some hotels.

TIPPING

Beijing is one of those places where tipping is not the norm. Porters in flash hotels will expect something, but waiters and taxi drives will be bemused if you add on a tip and will often run after you to give it back. However, some swish restaurants do tack on a 10% to 15% service charge, as do all four- and five-star hotels.

TOURIST INFORMATION

It remains a mystery why Beijing's tourist information centres have yet to undergo the makeover so many other services in the city have received. Most staff have very limited English and little understanding of the needs of foreigners when it comes to tours and advice. There is a **Beijing Tourism Hotline** (☎ 6513 0828; ☷ 24hr) with English-speaking operators (press '1' after dialling the number) to answer questions and take complaints, but your best source of information will be your accommodation and other travellers. See also p153.

TRAVELLERS WITH DISABILITIES

Beijing is a challenge for anyone with limited mobility. There are few elevators (lifts), plus escalators in subway stations usually only go up (although some of the new stations do have lifts). Streets are overcrowded and uneven, forcing wheelchair users onto the road itself. Getting around sights and temples is not easy either – there are few ramps. Toilets marked 'wheelchair accessible' may be missing handrails or won't accommodate standard chair dimensions.

Travellers with sight, hearing or mobility disabilities will also need to be extremely cautious of the traffic, which does not yield to pedestrians. It's best to contact your local disability association for advice before you travel.

NOTES

>INDEX

See also separate subindexes for Drink (p166), Eat (p166), Play (p167), See (p167) and Shop (p168).

000 map pages

DRINK

EAT

000 map pages

000 map pages